LARRAINE S HARRISON

Published by Scholastic Ltd,
Villiers House,
Clarendon Avenue,
Leamington Spa,
Warwickshire CV32 5PR
Text © Larraine S Harrison
© 1999 Scholastic Ltd
1 2 3 4 5 6 7 8 9 0   9 0 1 2 3 4 5

AUTHOR
LARRAINE S HARRISON

EDITOR
LORNA GILBERT

ASSISTANT EDITOR
CLARE MILLER

SERIES DESIGNER
LYNNE JOESBURY

DESIGNERS
PETER JORDAN & LYNNE JOESBURY

ILLUSTRATIONS
ANN JOHNS

COVER ILLUSTRATION
JONATHAN BENTLEY

INFORMATION TECHNOLOGY CONSULTANT
MARTIN BLOWS

SCOTTISH 5–14 LINKS
MARGARET SCOTT AND SUSAN GOW

Designed using Adobe Pagemaker

British Library Cataloguing-in-Publication Data
A catalogue record for this book is available from the
British Library.

ISBN 0-590-53784-9

The right of Larraine S Harrison to be identified as the Author of this
work has been asserted by her in accordance with the Copyright,
Designs and Patents Act 1988.

Contents

INTRODUCTION 5

Overview grid 9

LANGUAGE AND LITERACY 13

ACTING FOR AN AUDIENCE 41

PERSONAL AND SOCIAL DEVELOPMENT 63

CROSS-CURRICULAR THEMES 89

PHOTOCOPIABLES 117

IT links 158

Cross-curricular links 160

Introduction

Scholastic Curriculum Bank is a series for all primary teachers, providing an essential planning tool for devising comprehensive schemes of work as well as an easily accessible and varied bank of practical, classroom-tested activities with photocopiable resources.

Designed to help planning for and implementation of progression, differentiation and assessment, *Scholastic Curriculum Bank* offers a structured range of stimulating activities with clearly stated learning objectives that reflect the programmes of study, and detailed lesson plans that allow busy teachers to put ideas into practice with the minimum amount of preparation time. The photocopiable sheets that accompany many of the activities provide ways of integrating purposeful application of knowledge and skills, differentiation, assessment and record-keeping.

Opportunities for formative assessment are highlighted within the activities where appropriate. Ways of using information technology for different purposes and in different contexts, as a tool for communicating and handling information and as a means of investigating, are integrated into the activities where appropriate, and more explicit guidance is provided at the end of the book.

The series covers all the primary curriculum subjects, with separate books for Key Stages 1 and 2 or Scottish Levels A–B and C–E. It can be used as a flexible resource with any scheme, to fulfil National Curriculum and Scottish 5–14 requirements and to provide children with a variety of different learning experiences that will lead to effective acquisition of skills and knowledge.

SCHOLASTIC CURRICULUM BANK ENGLISH

The *Scholastic Curriculum Bank English* books enable teachers to plan comprehensive and structured coverage of the primary English curriculum, and enable pupils to develop the required skills, knowledge and understanding through activities.

Each book contains one key stage. There are six books for Key Stage 1/Scottish levels A–B and six for Key Stage 2/Scottish levels C–E. These books reflect the English programme of study, so that there are titles on Reading, Writing, Speaking and listening and Spelling and phonics. The titles on Drama and Poetry cover all four aspects of the programme of study in relation to these subjects.

Bank of activities

This book provides a bank of activities which are designed to broaden children's experience of drama and enable them to develop their confidence and skill in working in drama.

Lesson plans

Detailed lesson plans, under clear headings, are given for each activity and provide material for immediate implementation in the classroom. The structure for each activity is as follows.

Activity title box

The information contained in the box at the beginning of each activity outlines the following key aspects:

▲ *Activity title and learning objective.* For each activity a clearly stated learning objective is given in bold italics. These learning objectives break down aspects of the programmes of study for English and The National Literacy Strategy's *Framework for Teaching* into manageable, hierarchical teaching and learning chunks, and their purpose is to aid planning for progression. These objectives can be linked to the National Curriculum and Scottish 5–14 requirements by referring to the overview grid at the end of this chapter (pages 9–12).

▲ *Class organization/Likely duration.* Icons ✝✝ and 🕐 signpost the suggested group sizes for each activity and the approximate amount of time required to complete it. Some activities are written to cover two or more sessions, and you may choose to extend other activities into more than one session if appropriate.

Previous skills/knowledge needed

Information is given here when it is necessary for the children to have acquired specific knowledge or skills prior to carrying out the activity.

Key background information

The information in this section outlines the main area of study and focuses on any particular teaching points that need to be addressed.

Preparation

Advice is given for those occasions when it is necessary for the teacher to carry out preparations for the activity. These often include preparing materials or making an appropriate setting for the drama.

Resources needed

All of the materials needed to carry out the activity are listed, so that the pupils or the teacher can gather them together easily before the beginning of the teaching session.

What to do

Easy-to-follow, step-by-step instructions are given for carrying out the activity, including suggestions for questions and discussion, as well as how to start and stop the drama when appropriate.

Suggestion(s) for extension/support

Ideas are given for ways of providing easy differentiation where activities lend themselves to this purpose. In all cases, suggestions are provided as to ways in which each activity can be modified for less able or extended for more able children.

Assessment opportunities

Where appropriate, opportunities for ongoing teacher assessment of the children's work during or after a specific activity are highlighted.

Opportunities for IT

Where opportunities for IT present themselves, these are briefly outlined with reference to particularly suitable types of program. The chart on page 159 presents specific areas of IT covered in the activities, together with more detailed support on how to apply particular types of program. Selected lesson plans serve as models for other activities by providing more comprehensive guidance on the application of IT; these lesson plans are indicated by bold page numbers on the grid and the ⬦ icon at the start of an activity.

Performance ideas

For many drama activities, a performance is an appropriate outcome rather than (or as well as) a display. In these cases, a range of performance activities are suggested, often based on the previous drama work that has been done.

Display ideas

Where they are relevant and innovative, display ideas are incorporated into activity plans.

Reference to photocopiable sheets

Where activities include photocopiable activity sheets, small reproductions of these are included in the lesson plans together with guidance notes for their use.

Assessment

Assessment of drama is more subjective than for reading and writing and progression is often more spiral than linear. Nevertheless it is important to have a general overview of children's attainment in drama in order to inform future planning. We need to consider the children both as individuals and as a class and keep simple records to assess children's drama skills and associated social skills. For example their ability to respond appropriately in role and participate in a range of drama activities with confidence and integrity are important, along with children's ability to work together within a dramatic context.

Much of the assessment will be similar to that employed to assess speaking and listening, but with the added dimension of role-play performance. Particular points to note for assessment are included for each activity.

▲ Devising skills: the ability to shape the material and plan and predict outcomes; to contribute ideas and develop the ideas of others; to negotiate; to recognize problems and consider the effectiveness of different styles of presentation.

▲ Performance skills: the ability to communicate effectively and imaginatively in role through speech and movement; to evaluate a piece of drama using appropriate theatre vocabulary.

▲ Spontaneous role-play: the ability to respond appropriately in role; to identify implications within the role-play; to initiate and sustain a line of thought in relation to the content of the drama; to have confidence in using and responding to a variety of different drama strategies; to understand and use symbolic representations in drama.

Photocopiable sheets

Many of the activities are accompanied by photocopiable sheets. Drama is essentially a practical subject, but there are many occasions when a photocopiable sheet can be used to prepare for an activity, to focus on an aspect of the work during the drama, or as a conclusion. Other sheets are intended to be used as a resource for the teacher to use in conjunction with specific activities. The sheets provide purposeful activities that are ideal for assessment and can be kept as records in pupils' portfolios of work.

Cross-curricular links

Cross-curricular links are identified on a simple grid which cross references the particular areas of study in English to the programmes of study for other subjects in the curriculum (see page 160).

DRAMA

Using drama with young children can be a rewarding experience and one which children often remember for a long time afterwards. It works alongside free play in the infant school and provides a more structured way of extending learning through the world of the imagination.

Drama provides a powerful and effective way of learning but many teachers lack the confidence to use it in their teaching. Some are cautious due to misguided views on what drama in the curriculum actually involves. There are many who define drama purely as putting on plays and those who restrict it to movement activities or setting up imaginary situations in the role play area. Drama certainly includes these things but it can be so much more. This book suggests different kinds of drama activities which involve using drama both as a teaching method and as an art form in its own right. The chapters reflect four important areas where drama can support children's learning: Language and Literacy, Acting for an Audience, Personal and Social Development and Cross-curricular Themes.

The activities in this book include simple ideas for teachers who have little or no previous experience in using drama, as well as ideas for the more confident teachers. Strategies range from simple freeze-frames depicting a single moment to more ambitious use of teacher-in-role.

Teacher-in-role

Attempting teacher-in-role for the first time can be a daunting prospect for the inexperienced teacher. This book includes advice on how to set things up properly, so that everyone understands what is happening.

Teacher-in-role is one of the most powerful drama strategies and one of the most effective in engaging children on an emotional level. It has the potential to present information and issues from a personal perspective and allows the teacher to work from inside the imaginary situation. A sincerity of approach is more important than great acting skills when taking on a role. Avoid behaving, speaking or wearing costumes that could frighten or amuse the children and plan what you will say carefully.

substitutes for reality. Sometimes, the contract includes details of what is to follow. Knowing something of what will happen in the drama gives young children a sense of security and an understanding of what will be expected of them. The contract is not meant to be a formal procedure but if a child should refuse to agree to enter the imaginary world, then you should offer that child an alternative. The way you respond will depend upon why you feel the child is refusing. If you feel that a child is genuinely anxious about the work, then let them observe until they feel they want to join in. If you feel that a child is refusing in order to receive attention, explain that children who can't agree to pretend have to sit out and watch or do other work at the side of the room. Briefly offer them this option and then carry on with the lesson.

Loss of control can be another factor preventing teachers from using drama. This can be a very real fear when working with enthusiastic children. The methods in this book have been selected to ensure that young children understand the rules and know the boundaries of behaviour when working in drama. The activities are tightly structured so that tasks are clear and the children know what is expected of them. The structure gives children the freedom to respond to drama in a constructive way, so that they are left feeling satisfied with their efforts rather than over-excited or confused. Most of the drama lessons are introduced according to a common pattern, involving making a contract and defining the space.

Making the contract

Making a 'contract to pretend' represents an agreement between the teacher and the children to enter into the imaginary world of the drama and to behave appropriately. Drama is essentially a narrative art form and is best explained to young children through the phrase 'pretending to be in a story'. Most young children understand the implications of what this means, especially as they often describe their own play in these terms. This simple phrase will suggest certain expectations to the children, which involve behaving as if the events were real and accepting that props, costumes and areas of the room can be

If children break the contract by behaving inappropriately during the drama, stop the work and renegotiate the contract by offering them the choice to sit out or join in properly. Children usually enjoy drama and the majority will have no problems in agreeing to the contract.

Defining the space

When working in a hall or large space, always make sure that the children understand which areas of the room are to be used for the drama. This can avoid problems once the drama starts. If the children are new to drama work or have not used the room before, it is wise to be very specific about areas that are out of bounds and equipment that must not be touched. Specify areas such as PE stores and stage areas and mention the need to avoid pianos, computers, music trolleys, wall bars and any other equipment that may be in the room. If children stray into these areas during the drama, have a quiet word with the offenders or stop the drama and remind the class where they should or should not be working.

Not all teachers have regular or frequent access to a hall for drama work. Many of the suggestions in this book are designed to take place in a classroom environment, where a small acting area is used as the definition of the drama space.

Learning objective	PoS/AO	Content	Type of activity	Page
Language and literacy				
To introduce freeze-frames, speaking thoughts and forum theatre.	Sp & List: 1a, d. Reading: 2c. ***English Language 5–14*** *Talking about texts: Level A.*	Pupils depict moments from a story using freeze-frames.	Whole class directing small groups.	14
To use physical theatre to consolidate learning.	Sp & List: 1d. Reading: 2b. ***Expressive Arts 5–14*** *Using movement and mime: Level A.*	Using body shapes to represent initial letter sounds in children's names.	Whole class and pairs work moving in a space.	15
To introduce teacher-in-role and hot-seating in relation to a story.	Sp & List: 1d, 2b. Reading: 2c. *Evaluating and appreciating: Level A.*	Listening to, questioning and speaking as characters from a selected story.	Whole class, paired and group asking and answering questions to develop notions of character.	17
To introduce and develop confidence in using physical theatre within a story context.	Sp & List: 1d. *Using movement and mime: Level A.*	Pupils listen to a story about clocks and respond appropriately in role.	Whole class interpreting a story through movement.	19
To use action/freeze narration and mime to sequence a story.	Sp & List: 1d, 2c. *As above.*	Pupils take on the roles of characters from a chosen story and mime the events in sequence.	Whole class discussing and miming a narrative.	21
To introduce the concept of whole-group drama using a traditional story.	Sp & List: 1d. Reading: 2c. *As above.*	Pupils take an imaginary journey to engage with the characters and events in a selected story.	Whole class miming a journey together, on wich they help a fictional character.	23
To build confidence in speaking and listening in role.	Sp & List: 1d, 2a. *Talking about experiences, feelings and opinions: Level A.*	Pupils take on the role of experts to plan and make a garden for Snow White, followed by talking on an imaginary radio show.	Whole class planning, miming and speaking within an imaginary situation.	28
To use detailed mime to illustrate instructions.	Sp & List: 1d, 2a. *Using movement and mime: Level A.*	Pupils help a confused puppet by miming simple procedures such as baking or changing for a PE lesson.	Whole class miming together.	31
To build confidence in paired improvisation.	Sp & List: 1a, 1d. *Talking about experiences, feelings and opinions: Level A.*	Pupils improvise a telephone conversation concerning a lost dog.	Whole class activity and pairs speaking in role.	33
To act out parts of a story through dance drama.	Sp & List: 1d. Reading: 1d. *Using movement and mime: Level B.*	Pupils explore and express a part of the story of Rama and Sita through movement.	Whole class taking part in movement.	35

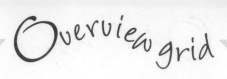

Learning objective	PoS/AO	Content	Type of activity	Page
To use whole-group drama to act out a well-known story.	Sp & List: 1d. Reading: 2c. *As above.*	Pupils acting out the full story of the Pied Piper.	Whole class and groups working in role.	37
Acting for an audience				
To develop skills in using movement and expression in role.	Sp & List: 1d. *Expressing, communicating and presenting: Level B.*	Pupils walking as characters feeling a variety of emotions in different situations. Building character around different objects.	Whole class activity and small groups moving together.	42
To develop confidence in the use of mime by performing simple activities.	Sp & and List: 1d. *Using movement and mime: Level A.*	Focusing on mime, building up from simple activities through to more challenging mime work.	Whole class and pairs miming and performing.	44
To build confidence in speaking in a different voice before an audience.	Sp & List: 1d. *Talking in groups: Level A.*	Using a games context to give children opportunities to practise using different voices.	Whole class and pairs experimenting with different voices.	45
To move from structured dramatic play to performance.	Sp & List: 1d. *Expressing, communicating and presenting: Level B.*	Children engage in dramatic play on the theme of a day out and adapt their ideas for performance in groups.	Whole class engaging in role-plays, then performing in groups.	47
To give practice in paired improvisations and responding as an audience.	Sp & List: 1a, b, c, d. *As above.*	Performing and responding to improvisations based on shopping.	Whole class and pairs miming and talking in role, leading to short performances in groups.	49
To develop freeze-frames into improvisations.	Sp & List: 1a, b, d *As above.*	Children bring freeze-frame pictures to life and then perform their improvisations to each other.	Whole class and small groups improvising from a given point of focus.	52
To use simple objects as props to stimulate spontaneous improvisation.	Sp & List: 1a, d. *As above.*	Acting out simple stories based around objects picked from a box. Each group performs to the rest of the class.	Whole class and small groups devising and acting out stories.	54
To build confidence in performing to a large audience.	Sp & List: 1d. *As above.*	Rehearsing the chosen play focusing on learning lines and projecting the voice effectively.	Small groups performing to the whole class.	55
To give practice in manipulating puppets for performance.	Sp & List: 1d. *As above.*	Practise moving simple hand puppets in a variety of ways. Each group performs to the rest of the class.	Small groups demonstrating to the whole class.	58
To extend children's understanding of theatre in preparation for a theatre visit.	Sp & List: 1d. *As above.*	An introduction to aspects of the theatre is followed by children creating model stages with sets and drawing various costumes.	Whole class and small groups engaged in practical work in music and art.	60

Learning objective	PoS/AO	Content	Type of activity	Page
Personal and social development				
To use an imaginary context to stimulate improvisation on personal and social issues.	Sp & List: 1a, d. 2b. **Religious and Moral Education** *Relationships: Level A.*	Giving advice to a puppet with a problem using role play.	Whole class giving advice. Groups acting out solutions.	64
To enable children to use freeze-frames as a focus for dicussion.	Sp & List: 1a, c, d. *As above.*	Listening to a simple story about bullying. The class explore solutions which are then recreated using freeze-frames.	Whole class directing small groups.	66
To develop group co-operation skills using a drama game.	Sp & List: 1d. *As above.*	Children use co-operation skills to help each other overcome imaginary problems.	Whole class involved in a movement game.	69
To support drama work by developing group awareness and identity.	Sp & List: 1d. *Personal and Social Development.*	Playing a game based on knowledge and observation within the group.	Whole class playing a circle game.	71
To support drama work by developing group co-operation skills and awareness.	Sp & List: 1d. *As above.*	Copying the movements of appointed leaders of the group.	Whole class following the actions of a leader.	73
To encourage children to work as a group to act out a simple story.	Sp & List: 1d. *As above.*	Miming a story about a young girl who plants some flowers in her grandad's bare garden.	Whole class miming appropriate actions for a story.	74
To encourage children to work collaboratively in role.	Sp & List: 1d. *As above.*	Mime and role-play on the theme of helping out on a farm.	Whole class and pairs using mime and role-play.	76
To enable children to explore issues of friendship within a dramatic context.	Sp & List: 1a, b, c, d. Writing: 1b, c. *As above.*	Drama in which pupils play the roles of servants and advisers to a young prince who cannot make friends.	Whole class and small groups acting together.	80
To provide an opportunity to take part in a whole-group drama about helping others.	Sp & List: 1d. **Expressive Arts 5–14** *Using movement and mime: Level A.*	An imaginary journey to help out in Santa's toy shop.	Whole class working in role with the teacher.	84
To focus on co-operating with a partner in an imaginary context.	Sp & List: 1d, 2b. *Expressing thoughts and ideas: Level B.*	Taking turns to imitate robots and give instructions on movements to cross an obstacle course.	Whole class and pairs negotiating a specified space.	87
Cross-Curricular Themes				
To use freeze-frames to depict and compare aspects of life in the past and present	Sp & List: 1a, d, 2a. History: Key elements 2c. **Environmental Studies 5–14** *Social subjects. People in the past: Level B.*	Using artefacts as a stimulus for exploring an aspect of life, such as washday, then and now.	Whole class and small groups freeze-framing past and present moments as a stimulus for comparison of the two.	90

Learning objective	PoS/AO	Content	Type of activity	Page
To develop confidence in making sound effects for drama.	Sp & List: 1d. Reading: 2c. Music: 5g. **Expressive Arts 5–14** *Using movement and mime: Level A.*	Acting out and making sound effects for a chosen story.	Whole class and small groups exploring ways to use music and sound to complement a drama.	92
To use whole-group role-play to focus on a geographical theme.	Sp & List: 1a, d. Geography: 5c. *As above.*	Role-play activity on the theme of taking a walk on a windy day.	Whole class working in role with the teacher.	94
To use teacher-in-role to stimulate role play on a historical theme.	Sp & List: 1a, 2b. History: Key Elements 2a, b, c. *Social subjects. People in the past: Level C.*	Teacher playing the role of a child in the Second World War. The class talk to the child and then play the part of prospective evacuees.	Whole class activity with small group work	97
To perform a dance drama on a religious theme.	Sp & List: 1d. *Using movement: Level B.*	Using movement to act out part of the Christmas story.	Whole class exploring the Christmas story through movement and dance.	102
To give children an opportunity to take on roles of responsibility within a dramatic context.	Sp & List: 1a, c, d. Geography: 3d. *Expressing, communicating and presenting: Level B.*	Creating and miming working in an imaginary wildlife park, helping to overcome a litter problem.	Whole class and small groups working in role.	105
To use whole-group drama to enable children to express their understanding of health issues.	Sp & List: 1a, d, 2a. Science: 2.2c. *As above.*	Drama requiring the children to help the old woman who lives in a shoe to provide a healthy diet for her children.	Whole class and pairs working in role with the teacher.	108
To use whole-group drama as a context for mathematical tasks.	Sp & List: 1d, 2a. Maths: 3.2. **Mathematics 5–14** *Shape, position and movement.*	Planning an imaginary garden on a shapes theme and sorting 3D shapes to make models.	Whole class, pairs and individuals discussing and planning in a role-play situation.	111
To use whole-group drama to introduce children to a historical figure.	Sp & List: 1d. History: Areas of Study 2. **Environmental Studies 5–14** *Understanding earth and space: Level B.*	Imagining going back in time to help on Isaac Newton's farm, and then exploring gravity in space and on earth.	Whole class and pairs working in role with the teacher.	113
To use physical theatre to represent numbers and simple sums.	Speaking and Listening: 1d. Maths: 2.1c **Mathematics 5–14** *Number, money, measure. Shape, position and movement: Level B.*	Using the body to make number shapes and simple mathematical signs.	Whole class using their bodies to reinforce number recognition and record sums.	115

Entries given in italics relate to the following Scottish National guidelines: English Language 5–14, Expressive Arts 5–14, Religious and Moral Education, Environmental Studies and Mathematics 5–14.

DRAMA

Language and literacy

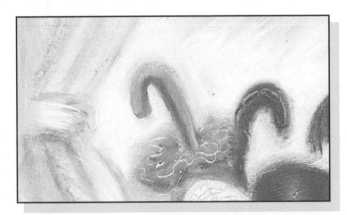

Drama provides a range of enjoyable and stimulating contexts for language. Stepping inside an imaginary situation introduces the children to new relationships, which in turn make new language demands. The roles of responsibility and expertise that they can take on in drama go far beyond anything the children could manage in real life. This raises expectations, enabling them to experience different language registers and to speak for a range of audiences.

Children also have the opportunity through drama to look at familiar stories and rhymes from the point of view of a participant. This brings the text to life and encourages a deeper understanding. The children's ability to visualize a story or rhyming text is also supported, giving important messages that reading is about making meaning. Such work can be a great asset in the drive to improve literacy.

Experiencing a story in drama can also stimulate and improve the quality of the children's creative writing. They can benefit greatly through the opportunities provided to write for a range of different audiences. Another advantage is that the motivation for writing arises from the stories or rhymes themselves, rather than writing for its own sake or to please the teacher.

This chapter provides a range of drama activities designed to extend the children's language, stimulate written work and increase their appreciation of literature. There are opportunities to analyse and reflect upon particular moments in a story, look closely at letter shapes, take part in stories both old and new and give information and instructions.

DRAMA

SPECIAL MOMENTS

To introduce freeze-frames, speaking thoughts and forum theatre.

†† *Small groups performing to the whole class.*

🕐 *30 minutes.*

Previous skills/knowledge needed

It will be helpful if the children have some experience in moving and 'freezing' in different positions on a given signal. They will also need to know the sequence of events in the chosen story or rhyme.

Key background information

This activity can take place in the classroom. It focuses on significant moments in a well-known story or rhyme which the children are invited to depict in a 'freeze-frame'. This provides a visual focus for reflection on and analysis of each moment under observation. The activity depends on the teacher asking structured questions which require the children to consider each moment from different perspectives. The class are invited to make key decisions as a group, introducing a simple version of forum theatre.

Preparation

Select a moment from a familiar story or rhyme that has potential for discussion. For example, the moment when Humpty Dumpty sat on the wall, the moment when Goldilocks ran away from the Bears or the moment when the Gingerbread Man jumped out of the oven. Collect one item of clothing for each character in the selected moment. Choose items that are easy to take on and off, such as scarves or aprons with Velcro fastenings. Read the chosen rhyme or story with the children to make sure that they are familiar with the sequence of events.

Draw and cut out an A4-sized thought bubble from a piece of card. Make one copy per child of photocopiable page 118. Clear a small space for an acting area at the front of the classroom.

Resources needed

Photocopiable page 118, chosen text, thought bubble, items of clothing (see above), a sheet of A4 card, scissors, writing materials.

What to do

Introduction: Practising a freeze

Ask some children to stand at the front of the classroom and make sure that everyone can see them. Explain that you need them to stand very still, or 'freeze', as if they were in a picture from the chosen story or rhyme (see 'Preparation'). Let them practise this first freeze, then ask them to try other frozen positions such as running, climbing a ladder or eating a sandwich. Stress the need to keep very still, as if frozen on a video freeze-frame.

Development: Making a freeze-frame

Ask each child at the front to put on the costume for their character. Then ask the class a series of questions to help

DRAMA

make key decisions about the freeze-frame (this is a version of forum theatre). Begin by establishing where each character might be looking. Try to suggest alternatives, for example: *Is Goldilocks looking into the forest as she runs away, or is she looking at the mess she left behind?* Other questions might include how the characters are feeling, for example: *Is Humpty Dumpty feeling happy when he sits on the wall or does he think he might fall? Is he smiling or looking scared?* Ask the class to show the characters how to make the appropriate facial expressions. The amount of time spent on the questioning will depend on the concentration levels of the class.

The characters must now make the final freeze-frame, incorporating the suggestions made by the class. The characters must freeze when you say the word 'Freeze', and hold their positions to the count of three before relaxing.

Conclusion: Speaking thoughts
Give each child a copy of photocopiable page 118. Invite their suggestions on what the character in the first picture might be thinking. Encourage different interpretations and accept all versions as long as they are genuine and sensible. Now ask the children to think about the next picture. Let them talk to a partner about their ideas before discussing possibilities as a whole class. Repeat this sequence with the other pictures. Ask the children to write their suggestions in the thought bubbles on the sheet before reporting back to the whole class.

Now ask the children at the front to make the freeze-frame as before. Hold the A4 thought bubble (see 'Preparation') in turn above each character's head and ask the class what each character might be thinking.

Suggestion(s) for extension
Ask confident children in the freeze-frame to speak out a thought for their character when the bubble is placed over their head. They can use suggestions from the class or make up their own thoughts.

Suggestion(s) for support
Look at real pictures of the story before making the freeze-frame. Ask less confident children to help you choose and put out a few simple props to set the scene. Pair up less confident children with those who are more able when working on the photocopiable sheet.

What are they thinking?

Name _____ Date _____

▲Use the speech bubbles to write each character's thoughts.

Humpty Dumpty

Baby Bear

Little Miss Muffett

The third Little Pig

Assessment opportunities
Note which children are able to make and sustain an appropriate position within the freeze-frame. Look for children who are confident at performing in front of others and for those who can look beyond the sequence of events in the story to consider the characters' feelings.

Performance ideas
Narrate a story, stopping at various points to let groups of children illustrate the narrative by performing freeze-frames. The children can dress up in costumes and use a few props to make the freeze-frames look more realistic. These can be rehearsed and performed to a wider audience, such as the rest of the school or parents.

Display ideas
Record the freeze frames in photographs or drawings. Make speech bubbles from sticky paper and add to the photographs or drawings to make a display.

Reference to photocopiable sheet
Photocopiable page 118 can be used to introduce the concept of thought bubbles to the children.

SOUND SHAPES

To use physical theatre to consolidate learning.
†† *Whole class and pairs.*
🕐 *30 minutes.*

Previous skills/knowledge needed
The children need to feel happy about working physically with a partner. They should also be familiar with capital letter shapes and their sounds.

Key background information
Physical theatre is used in this activity to consolidate learning about capital letter shapes and their sounds. The work is designed to be completed during a single lesson but can be extended over several if necessary. The activity can be adapted to focus on final sounds in various words.

Preparation
Make one copy of photocopiable page 119 per pair of children. Write a list of simple first names with clear initial sounds, such as Tom, Matthew, Alice, Lorna, Amrit, Dean,

DRAMA

Emma, Faye, Hannah. Place a large alphabet chart where all the children can easily see it.

Resources needed
Photocopiable page 119, a large alphabet chart showing upper and lower case letters, writing materials, a large space.

What to do
Introduction and demonstration
Explain to the children that the capital letters used for people's names are called initials.

Give out photocopiable page 119 and let the children work in pairs to complete it. They should use the alphabet chart to help them if necessary.

When most of the children have finished, ask them to look carefully at the capital letters they have written for David Harrison's initials. Ask one child to make up a pair with you at the front and then demonstrate how to make

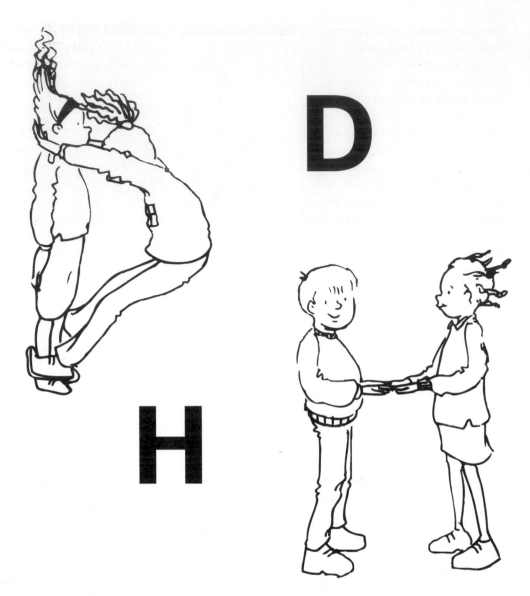

the initial letters 'D' and then 'H' using your bodies. For example, the letter 'D' can be made with one partner lying out straight on the floor and the other curving their body. 'H' can be made by standing opposite your partner and joining outstretched hands in the middle.

Now ask the children to look at the initials for Joanne Rutledge. Invite two volunteers to come to the front and make the shapes of these initials with their bodies. Encourage suggestions from the class on how to do this if necessary. Let different pairs take turns to demonstrate the other initials on the sheet.

Development: Making letter shapes
When you feel the children understand the process, ask them to find a space in the hall with their partners. They should then work out how to perform their own initials using their bodies as demonstrated before. Make it clear that they should work out how to make both sets of initials, trying four to six letters. They can refer to the alphabet chart again to remind them of the correct shapes.

When everyone has worked out how to perform at least one set of initials, stop the class. Ask each pair to choose

two of their letter shapes to show the class. Give them a few minutes to practise, then let them perform their letters after telling the class what these letters are. Point out any differences in the way the same letters are performed. Make constant reference to the alphabet chart to check the shapes.

Conclusion: Responding to initial letter sounds
Explain that you are going to read out some first names. When the children hear a name, they must work with their partners to perform the initial letter of that name as quickly as they can. Give an example by saying the name 'Tom' twice, emphasizing the 't' sound to indicate the letter they should perform. When the children are ready, read out the names one at a time and ask them to make the initial letters. They will respond at different rates but try to wait until all the pairs have made some attempt at the letter before asking a child to name it.

Suggestion(s) for extension
Give more confident children a short list of simple place names and ask them to make the words with their bodies.

They can achieve this by performing the words one letter at a time, using capital and lower case letter shapes in the appropriate places.

Suggestion(s) for support
Encourage less confident children to make the shapes of their initials before the drama lesson, using a range of materials such as sand, dough and paint. Give them plastic letters representing their initials and let them work near the alphabet chart when making the shapes. Put less confident children with more confident pairs during the concluding part of the activity.

Assessment opportunities
Look for children who show confidence and imagination when using the body to represent the shapes. The ability to discriminate between the shapes of letters can also be observed.

Display ideas
Take photographs of the children making whole words with their letter shapes. This will look more effective if the children are wearing clothes of the same colour. In this way, they can create words for notices or signs such as 'Welcome to Our School'.

Reference to photocopiable sheet
Photocopiable page 119 focuses on the skill of identifying initials from names. It is used as a common reference point when demonstrating the technique at the start of the activity.

FROM MY POINT OF VIEW

To introduce teacher-in-role and hot-seating in relation to a story.

†† *Whole class, pairs and groups.*

🕐 *30 to 45 minutes.*

Previous skills/knowledge needed
The children should be familiar with the characters and sequence of events in the chosen story.

Key background information
Teacher-in-role can provide a model of good practice that sets the tone for hot-seating and other drama work. This activity begins with the teacher playing a character from a story and finishes with an opportunity for the children to hot-seat in groups.

When working in role, the teacher needs to present an attitude with sincerity rather than putting on a superficial act. Your role must be planned carefully so that you are clear about what you want to achieve. When telling a story in role, it is often helpful to memorize the first and last lines and to have some key points to assist your storytelling. Always make it clear when you are in role and when you are not.

This activity is intended to be completed during one lesson, but it can be spread over two if necessary.

Preparation
Make one copy per child of photocopiable page 120. Select a familiar story with four or more characters. Traditional stories such as 'The Three Billy Goats Gruff', 'The Three Bears' or 'The Three Little Pigs' are suitable examples.

scarf. Ask the children to listen carefully to what the character has to say to them. Then put on the scarf and tell the story in a colloquial manner, from your character's point of view. Take off the scarf to come out of role. Ask the children questions about what the character said and how the character felt, for example: *What did the builder think when the first pig asked him for some straw to build a house? How did the middle Billy Goat feel when he saw the little Billy Goat cross the bridge?*

Development: Thinking about a character

Ask the children if they will pretend to be other characters from the story. Explain that groups of children will pretend to be the same character and will take turns to talk to the class. Emphasize that they must think about their character carefully before they pretend.

Organize the class into three mixed-ability groups and pair children up within these groups. Then select three more characters from the same story and allocate one to each group. (Make sure the children are familiar with these characters.) Assign each group a character to play and then give each child a copy of photocopiable page 120. Read through the sheet with the class to make sure that everyone understands what to do. The children should fill in one sheet each but can work in pairs to help each other.

Conclusion: Hot-seating as a group

When most children have completed their sheets, stop the activity and select one group for hot-seating. Explain that this involves speaking and answering questions as if they were a character in the story. Groups need not come to the front for the hot-seating, but if possible they should sit together in one part of the room.

Start by discussing with the class what they might like to ask the character and decide on a few appropriate questions. Explain that the children in the hot-seat will take turns to speak as the character. You may have to ask the first few questions yourself, structuring them carefully to encourage a suitable reply. If the children still lack confidence, direct the proceedings by asking various children in the hot-seat to relate a particular part of the story. (Note that this activity is intended as an introduction to hot-seating and some classes will need further practice before they become confident.) Repeat the hot-seating with the other two groups in the same way. Conclude each hot-seating by summarizing what the class has discovered about the character.

Suggestion(s) for extension

Give more able children the opportunity to hot-seat a different character. Ask probing questions to encourage

Choose a character from the story to present to the children in role. If possible, this should be a more minor character who will bring a different perspective to the events, such as the middle Billy Goat Gruff, Mummy or Daddy Bear or the second Little Pig.

Alternatively, you can invent a character who would have knowledge of the events in the story, such as the builder who gave the straw, wood and bricks to the Three Pigs or a farmer who saw what happened to the Billy Goats from his farmhouse window.

Prepare an outline of the events in the story from your character's viewpoint. Try to focus on the character's feelings and observations.

Resources needed

Photocopiable page 120, drawing and writing materials, a simple item of clothing, such as a scarf, to represent your character, chair(s) for 'hot-seating'.

What to do

Introduction: Teacher-in-role

Remind the children of the selected story if necessary. Explain that you will pretend to be your chosen character from the story when you are wearing the scarf. Make it clear that you will stop pretending when you take off the

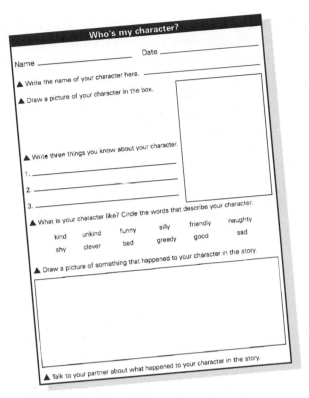

them to express their character's feelings about the events and relationships in the story.

Suggestion(s) for support

Put less confident children with pairs to make a group of three when completing the photocopiable sheet. Assign them to pairs who will support them with their work. Differentiate the questioning to include less confident children when they are in the hot-seat group.

Assessment opportunities

Look for signs of concentration and good listening when the children are responding to you during the teacher-in-role activity. Look for appropriate responses and any attempts at characterization when children are in the hot-seat. This activity also provides an opportunity to assess children's questioning skills.

Display ideas

Draw an outline of each of the chosen characters onto large sheets of paper. Write in each outline all the things the children discovered about that character during the hot-seating. This can take the form of single words or statements such as: 'Daddy Bear thinks Goldilocks should say sorry', or 'The huntsman didn't really want to leave Snow White in the woods.' Display these alongside the children's drawings of each character at various points in the story.

Reference to photocopiable sheet

Photocopiable page 120 is designed to help the children think about their character before they take the hot-seat.

THE CLOCKMAKER'S DREAM

To introduce and develop confidence in using physical theatre within a story context.

†† *Whole class.*

🕐 *20 to 30 minutes.*

Previous skills/knowledge needed

The children should know what old clocks look like. They should understand that larger clocks make different sounds to small clocks. Some previous experience of moving in response to a sound and of stopping on a given signal, such as the beat of a tambour, is also necessary.

Key background information

This activity requires the children to listen and behave appropriately in role using physical theatre. It is based around a story (see below) but the children need not be familiar with this beforehand. During the activity, the beat of a tambour is used as a signal for starting and stopping the movements each time. Responding accurately in this way is a more difficult skill for young children to acquire. It may be helpful to give them some initial practice before starting the lesson

DRAMA

Preparation

Learn the following storyline and decide how to tell it in your own words.

A clockmaker had a shop full of old clocks. He loved the clocks but they made him cross with all their noisy ticking and chiming. Every night, before going to bed, the clockmaker would wind them all up. One night, the clockmaker couldn't sleep because of the noisy clocks. He was so cross that he found a large hammer and broke all the clocks up.

The next morning, he felt very sad and regretted what he had done. He went downstairs to see if he could fix them. As he reached the door, he thought that he could hear the clocks ticking and chiming. When he opened the door, he was amazed to find that they were not broken after all. The clockmaker knew that it must have been a dream.

He was so pleased that he promised never to complain about the noisy clocks again. That night when he wound up the clocks, he gave them all a little polish to show how wonderful he thought they were.

Resources needed

A large space, a waistcoat or scarf to represent the clockmaker, a tambour.

What to do

Sit the children together at the side of the hall. Tell them the story of the clockmaker's dream and ask them a few questions to make sure that they understand it. Tell them that you will pretend to be the clockmaker when you are wearing the waistcoat (or scarf) and ask them if they will pretend to be the clocks. Ask them to think about what kind of clock they would like to be. Discuss some possibilities such as cuckoo clocks, grandfather clocks and alarm clocks. Talk about appropriate body shapes and discuss the kinds of sounds the clocks might make.

Stand the children in a large semi-circle or in rows. Make sure they have some space between them. Explain how you will use a beat on the tambour as a signal for stopping and starting the clock sounds, then give the children a few minutes to practise being the clocks. Choose one or two children to show the class their clock movements. Then divide the class into two and let each half perform their clock movements in turn.

Now go through the story again, using the tambour to indicate when you want the children to make the sounds. Stop the clock sounds when the children need to listen to the narrative. Mime the following actions as if you were the clockmaker: wind up each clock, break down each clock with a hammer (agree how the clocks should respond beforehand), listen outside the door, find the clocks in one piece, wind and polish each clock.

After the story, point out examples of good practice in physical theatre, such as stiff, straight arm or hand movements representing the clock hands or pendulum. Then repeat the activity, incorporating any of the children's suggestions for improvement.

Suggestion(s) for extension
When the class are making up their clock movements, let more confident children work in pairs to represent the body and hands of a large clock or a clock with different parts such as a cuckoo clock.

Suggestion(s) for support
When the class are making up their clock movements let less confident children work together in a group, either with you or another adult. Show them two or three pictures of different clocks and ask them to choose which one they will be. Talk about how each clock will sound and help the children make appropriate body shapes for their clocks.

Support those who find it difficult to stand as still as clocks in the story by asking them to be the clockmaker's assistants. They can accompany you as you wind up the clocks, perhaps winding some themselves if appropriate. They can then return to being clocks for the other parts of the story.

Assessment opportunities
Look for imaginative physical interpretations of the clocks. Check for evidence of good listening and appropriate responses to the story. Note those children who can stop and start on the given signal.

Display ideas
Ask each child to paint two pictures of their clock; one to illustrate the real clock and the other to illustrate the broken clock in the dream. Display the paintings of the real clocks as if they were in the shop window and display the 'dream' clocks inside a cloud shape, above an outline of the sleeping clockmaker.

Performance ideas
Teach the children to make the clock sounds in response to the narration, instead of using the tambour. Choose a confident child to be the clockmaker as you narrate the story. Dress the children in dark-coloured clothes or scarves to represent the clocks and perform the story to an audience.

SEQUENCING A STORY

To use action/freeze narration and mime to sequence a story.

†† *Whole class.*

🕐 *30 minutes.*

Previous skills/knowledge needed
Children need to be told the story selected for this activity before the lesson. Previous experience in making freeze-frames (see 'Special moments' on page 14) would be helpful.

Key Background information
This activity is closely linked to the idea of freeze-frames (see above). It allows the whole class to act out parts of a story within a controlled framework. At the same time, it gives children an opportunity to experience the sequence of events from the characters' perspectives. The activity also encourages the development of listening skills and the appropriate use of mime. The command words 'Action' and 'Freeze' are introduced here for starting and stopping the mime sequences.

Preparation

Photocopiable page 121 shows the sequence of activities in the story of 'Little Red Riding Hood' together with opportunities for mime. You can either copy this to base the lesson around or choose another familiar story and use the sheet as a guide to the structure. Note that each section of the chosen story should include between two and six mime activities. Write these sections out on paper using a similar structure to the photocopiable sheet.

Resources

Photocopiable page 121, writing materials or a word processor to prepare a copy of the story as above, a large space.

What to do

Introduction: Practising the 'Action/Freeze' technique

Ask the children to walk around the hall without touching anyone else. Instruct them to start when you say the word 'Action' and to stop like statues when you say the word 'Freeze'. Explain that they should remain in the frozen position until you tell them to sit down. Extend the activity by asking the children to walk in different directions such as backwards and sideways. Then ask them to travel in other ways such as skipping, hopping or jumping.

Now ask the children to walk as if they were different creatures or people each time. This might include walking as if they were mice, giants, marching soldiers, a parent pushing a baby buggy or a gardener pushing a wheelbarrow. Extend this by adding a purpose or feeling to the walking, such as a mouse looking for cheese, giants walking upstairs to bed, marching soldiers feeling tired, a parent in a hurry to get home or a gardener pushing a heavy wheelbarrow up a hill. Make sure that most of the children are able to respond to the words 'Action' and 'Freeze' appropriately before moving on to the story.

Development: Miming the story

Approach each section of the story in the following way: read out the section, tell the children which part you would like them to play, discuss how best to mime the chosen character's actions, ask for volunteers to demonstrate possibilities and decide on the final mimes. Make it clear that the children should mime only those actions which you have all agreed on.

Stress the need to listen carefully so that everyone knows what to do. For example, if the children are pretending to be Red Riding Hood walking through the forest, they must stop to pick some flowers when you say she left the path to pick some flowers. Emphasize that there may be moments without accompanying mime. Then, after completing all the story sections, perform them again without the intervening discussions.

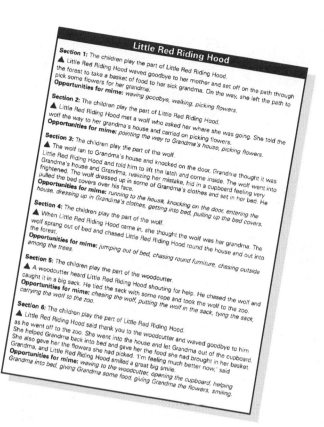

Little Red Riding Hood

Section 1: The children play the part of Little Red Riding Hood.
▲ Little Red Riding Hood waved goodbye to her mother and set off on the path through the forest to take a basket of food to her sick grandma. On the way, she left the path to pick some flowers for her grandma.
Opportunities for mime: *waving goodbye, walking, picking flowers.*

Section 2: The children play the part of Little Red Riding Hood.
▲ Little Red Riding Hood met a wolf who asked her where she was going. She told the wolf the way to her grandma's house and carried on picking flowers.
Opportunities for mime: *pointing the way to Grandma's house, picking flowers.*

Section 3: The children play the part of the wolf.
▲ The wolf ran to Grandma's house and knocked on the door. Grandma thought it was Little Red Riding Hood and told him to lift the latch and come inside. The wolf went into Grandma's house and Grandma, realizing her mistake, hid in a cupboard feeling very frightened. The wolf dressed up in some of Grandma's clothes and sat in her bed. He pulled the bed covers over his face.
Opportunities for mime: *running to the house, knocking on the door, entering the house, dressing up in Grandma's clothes, getting into bed, pulling up the bed covers.*

Section 4: The children play the part of the wolf.
▲ When Little Red Riding Hood came in, she thought the wolf was her grandma. The wolf sprang out of bed and chased Little Red Riding Hood round the house and out into the forest.
Opportunities for mime: *jumping out of bed, chasing round furniture, chasing outside among the trees.*

Section 5: The children play the part of the woodcutter.
▲ A woodcutter heard Little Red Riding Hood shouting for help. He chased the wolf and caught it in a big sack. He tied the sack with some rope and took the wolf to the zoo.
Opportunities for mime: *chasing the wolf, putting the wolf in the sack, tying the sack, carrying the wolf to the zoo.*

Section 6: The children play the part of Little Red Riding Hood.
▲ Little Red Riding Hood said thank you to the woodcutter and waved goodbye to him as he went off to the zoo. She went into the house and let Grandma out of the cupboard. She helped Grandma back into bed and gave her the food she had brought in her basket. She also gave her the flowers she had picked. 'I'm feeling much better now,' said Grandma, and Little Red Riding Hood smiled a great big smile.
Opportunities for mime: *waving to the woodcutter, opening the cupboard, helping Grandma into bed, giving Grandma some food, giving Grandma the flowers, smiling.*

Suggestion(s) for extension

For the final repeat of the story, give more confident children a few simple percussion instruments and talk about how they could be used to complement the mime in each section. Narrate the story, with these children being musicians in some sections and actors in others.

Suggestion(s) for support

Introduce less confident children to the 'Action' and 'Freeze' commands prior to the activity by using these words to start and stop everyday tasks in the classroom. Put less confident children in pairs to work alongside those who are more confident when miming the story.

Assessment opportunities

Assess the children's ability to listen and respond appropriately to the command words and the story. Look for children who show imagination in their use of mime and those who can perform with confidence and accuracy.

Performance ideas

Organize the children into groups and let each group mime a different section of the story as you narrate. Help the groups to rehearse and elaborate on their original mimes for a performance.

Reference to photocopiable sheet

Photocopiable page 121 can be used to sequence the miming of 'Little Red Riding Hood', or it can be used as an outline for sequencing a different story.

JOURNEY TO STORYLAND

To introduce the concept of whole-group drama using a traditional story.

👥 Whole class and pairs or threes.

🕐 45 minutes.

Previous skills/knowledge needed

The children need to be told the story used in the activity before the lesson takes place. The story is based around the house of the third Little Pig from the traditional tale 'The Three Pigs' (see main activity). The children should also know what a decorator does for a living.

Key background information

Whole-group drama is where all the children and the teacher behave as if they were inside the imaginary situation. They move through the narrative as if it were really happening. The skill lies in making the drama feel real, while at the same time acknowledging the pretence. This can be achieved through a combination of careful structuring and a sincere response to the imagined events.

Whole-group drama can create an opportunity for the children to sequence and reflect on events in the story from a personal perspective. This activity is based on the story of 'The Three Little Pigs', but any other familiar story can be used instead. In this example, the children go on a visit

to see the third Little Pig's new house, but when they arrive, they are asked to help with the decorating.

The structure of the activity allows the children to engage with the story on a personal level without changing the narrated events. This usually involves helping the characters with some practical task at the end of the story. For example, the children could go on a journey to the house of the Three Bears and tidy up the mess left by Goldilocks, or they could go on a journey to the dwarves' house and help to make food for a surprise wedding party for Snow White.

Preparation

Make single copies of photocopiable pages 122, 123, 124 and 125 and paste them onto separate pieces of A4 card. Place these pictures in individual plastic wallets and put them in order, starting with photocopiable page 122. Fasten the pictures together with treasury tags. Prepare a sign from A4 card saying 'Green Lane', and make one copy of the letter on photocopiable page 126.

Place the 'Green Lane' sign on a wall in the acting space and position the photocopiable letter near the sign but out of sight. Put the scarf and bucket in an inconspicuous place in the room. Write a thank you note from the third Little Pig, thanking the children for decorating his house (see 'What to do' below). Put this note away until after the activity.

Resources needed

Photocopiable pages 122–126, five sheets of A4 card, glue, four A4 plastic wallets, two treasury tags, writing materials, pictures and/or a book about decorating, a woollen scarf and a bucket, a 'thank you' card or note (see 'Preparation'), a large space.

What to do
Introduction: Practising the mimes
Show the children some pictures or books about decorating and talk about the jobs involved. Discuss how the jobs might be mimed, then organize the children into pairs or threes and let them practise miming these jobs.

Development: Telling the story
Sit the children in two or three rows facing into the hall, preferably opposite the 'Green Lane' sign. Make sure that everyone can see the sign. Ask the children if they will join you in pretending to go on a journey to storyland. Ask them to pretend that they have been invited to visit the third Little Pig's new brick house. Explain that it is quite safe to visit the house, now that the wolf has gone. Show them the picture of the house and lane and explain that the Pig's address is 3 Green Lane. Point out the sign on the picture and the sign on the wall and invite the children to pretend that the hall is Green Lane. Tell them which parts of the hall are to be used for the story.

Explain that your pictures will show the children what they need to pretend for the story. Show them the picture of the hat and scarf. Ask them to copy you as you pretend to put on these items. Do the same with the next picture of the coat. Now show the children the picture of the bus and explain that they will need to pretend to travel to Green Lane on a bus. Ask them to turn sideways, so that they are sitting in twos or threes, as if on bus seats.

Say that you are now ready to begin the story. Start by saying: *'Once upon a time, a group of children from this school went to storyland on a bus...and this is what happened...'.* To build up the children's belief in the imaginary context, you must now begin to talk and behave as if the events were really happening. Pretend to step onto the front of the bus and kneel or sit facing the children, as if you have your back to the driver's seat. Suggest that you all sing a song to pass the time. Choose an appropriate song such as 'The wheels on the bus' (*Action Rhymes* by Max de Bóo, Scholastic).

After singing the song, announce that the bus has arrived in Green Lane. Explain to the children that Green Lane is quite long, so they will have to walk for a while before they reach the brick house. Arrange them to stand with their partners in a crocodile formation before leading them along an imaginary route around the hall. Stop at various intervals to negotiate one or two obstacles such as crossing a narrow bridge, jumping over puddles or walking under the branches of overhanging trees.

Eventually, stop to announce that there is straw all over the lane. Explain that this is from the Little Pig's house of straw after the wolf blew it down. Ask the children to help you gather up the straw and put it in a nearby field. If you start to mime this as you speak, the children will join in without the need to stop the drama and explain what is required. Then notice a pile of wood in the lane. Explain that this is all that is left of the house of wood after the wolf blew it down. Talk about the danger of leaving pieces

of wood in the middle of a lane, then ask for help in moving the wood to the side of the road. Next, call the children together and tell them that the house of bricks is by the sign saying 'Green Lane'. Gather them to sit near the sign outside the imaginary brick house, then say that you will now tell them what happened next in the story.

Resume a narrative style to tell the next part of the story. Explain that when the children arrived at the third Little Pig's brick house, the door was open but no-one was in. The children then found a letter. Now bring out the letter (photocopiable page 126) and read it aloud to re-start the drama. Make it clear that the children must plan the decorating work carefully to do a good job for the Little Pig. Discuss what will be involved and decide what to do first. Use mime to demonstrate how to do the first job, then let the children mime this with their partners. Keep the task fairly short and then call the children to sit together while you inspect and praise the work.

Now discuss the other jobs that need doing, demonstrating them where necessary. The children should then carry these out with their partners as before. (Either allocate the jobs or let the children choose.) When some children appear to have finished, call everyone to sit together and go through each job to check that they have all been carried out. If a particular job has not been tackled, then let all the children carry it out. Walk round the house and praise the work.

DRAMA

Next, organize the children into pairs in an ordered formation as they were before, and retrace the route back to the bus. Sit everyone back on the bus a few at a time. Say that you are now going to tell them what happened next in the story. Move into a narrative style by saying: *'Just as the children were about to go home on the bus, someone came along the road and asked the driver if she/he could speak to the children.'* Explain that this person was wearing a scarf and carrying a bucket, then show them these

items. Say that you will pretend to be this person when you put on the scarf and pick up the bucket.

Now use the props to help you play the role of a decorator, wanting to know if the third Little Pig needs his new brick house decorating. Explain that you have tried to call the Pig but there was no reply. When the children tell you that the decorating has already been done, ask them to tell you exactly what they have done, just in case they have overlooked something.

Then say you have heard that another pig has built a new wooden house in Green Lane and you were wondering if he wanted it decorating. After the children have explained what happened to the wooden house, ask them if it's true that another pig tried to build a house of straw. Invite them to tell you what happened to this house if they have not already done so.

Finish by telling the children how kind they have been to decorate the brick house for the third Little Pig and then leave the bus. Put away the scarf and bucket and make it clear that you are now out of role. Step back onto the bus and ask the children to sing a song on the way home. Then ask everyone to face the front before telling them that this is the end of the story.

Conclusion: Reflection
Finish by asking individual children to pick out the things they liked best about the journey to storyland. Discuss the different jobs they did at the Little Pig's house and talk about how pleased he will be when he returns home. Some time after the activity, send the children a thank you note from the third Little Pig.

Suggestion(s) for extension
Before making the return bus journey, ask more confident children to describe the route back. What things do they see on the way? When you are in role as the decorator, invite these children to recall the details of how they did the decorating.

Suggestion(s) for support
Put less confident children in groups with those who will support and include them. Offer additional support by joining in with miming the decorating jobs. Ask these children to help you carry out your jobs or help them with theirs.

Assessment opportunities
Look for children who respond appropriately to the

DRAMA

imaginary context. Children's ability to retell a story in a different context can also be assessed as they attempt to tell the decorator what happened to the Little Pig's previous two houses. Confidence in working alongside others in a group context will also be evident.

Display ideas
Let the children help you to make a plan of the route to Green Lane. Display this alongside their pictures of the newly decorated house, a copy of the third Little Pig's letter and the thank you note. Let groups of children act out the

jobs they did in the drama and ask the rest of the class to guess what these are.

Reference to photocopiable sheets
Photocopiable pages 122, 123, 124 and 125 provide pictures to use as a resource when introducing the drama. Photocopiables 123–125 can be used on subsequent occasions when the class prepare to 'visit' the settings of other stories. Children will enjoy using familiar pictures for all journeys to storyland. Photocopiable page 129 provides a ready-made letter from the third Little Pig which can be adapted for other stories where a character needs help.

A GARDEN FOR SNOW WHITE

To build confidence in speaking and listening in role.

†† *Whole class.*

🕐 *Session One: 25 minutes. Session Two: 15 minutes.*

Previous skills/knowledge needed

The children should be familiar with the story of Snow White.

Key background information

The children take on the role of experts in this activity. This provides a good opportunity to motivate language and develop confidence in speaking in role. The activity is divided into two sessions which can be carried out in one lesson or spread over two. As Session Two relies on recall of the first session, the gap between them should not be too long.

Preparation

Make one copy of photocopiable page 127 and cut out the questions. Prepare a sign saying 'On Air' and create a cone-shape from a piece of thin A4 card. Write a thank you card from Snow White to the children expressing appreciation for their work in planning such a beautiful garden. Collect some pictures of large ornamental gardens and famous gardens belonging to stately homes. Attach temporarily two large sheets of light coloured sugar paper side by side on the wall to make one sheet.

Resources needed

Photocopiable page 127, pictures of large gardens, chalkboard or flip chart, scissors, drawing materials, glue, one sheet of paper per child (no larger than A3), two large sheets of light coloured sugar paper, Blu-Tack, two sheets of A4 card, a 'thank you' card (see above).

What to do
Session One

Sit the children so that they can see the board or flip chart and the sheets of sugar paper. Ask them to imagine that they are garden planners. Say that the Prince, in the story of Snow White, has asked them to plan out a large garden for Snow White, as a wedding present. The garden is to be made on some flat, grassy ground near the castle. They must plan the garden and send the Prince a drawing of what it will look like.

Show the children the pictures of the large gardens and discuss some possibilities for Snow White's garden. Emphasize the need to make it really special. Make a list of suggestions on the board. Organize these into categories, such as 'small flowers', 'rockery area', 'pool area', and

'steps', and mark them in pencil on the large sheet of sugar paper. Draw on any landmarks such as a path or a lawn.

Explain that the children are each going to draw a small part of the garden. Their drawings will then be pasted onto the sugar paper. Stress the need to make detailed pictures so that the gardeners will know what to do. Decide who will draw what so that all the features marked on the sugar paper are covered. Then give each child a sheet of paper no larger than A3 size. Ask them to cut out their drawing when it is finished.

Finish by pasting each contribution onto the sugar paper to create an overall picture of the garden. If you need more space, add another sheet of sugar paper. When the plan is finished, display it on the wall. Ask the children to imagine that a copy of the plan has been sent to the Prince.

Session Two

Tell the children that the Prince is very pleased with the plan and has told his gardeners to start work on making the garden. Say that there is great interest in the new garden and people have come from all over the kingdom to see its progress. In fact, everyone is so interested that the Prince has decided to set up a special radio station, so that people can write in with questions about the garden. The radio station is called 'Radio Palace'.

Ask the children to imagine that they have been invited to the Radio Palace studio to answer some questions sent in by the listeners. They should pretend that the classroom is the studio within which you will play the part of the radio presenter. Explain that the programme will start when you put up the sign saying 'On Air' (explain what this term means) and finish when you take the sign down. Ask them

to imagine that the paper cone is a radio microphone. Now put up the sign and take on the role of radio presenter. Make it clear that the garden is still in the process of being built as the programme goes on air. Then introduce the children as the planners, referring to them as 'special guests'.

Read out the questions one at a time from photocopiable page 127. Invite individual children to respond to these as you hand them the microphone. Make sure you stay in role as someone who knows nothing about the planning of the garden. Sign off by thanking your guests and commenting on how beautiful the garden will look when it is finished. Take down the sign to come out of role and finish the drama. Ask the children how they felt about being interviewed and discuss real life media interviews. Some time after the drama, send the children a thank you card from Snow White.

Suggestion(s) for extension

During Session One, ask more able children to include written descriptions of their ideas for the garden and any special instructions for the gardeners. In Session Two, allow the more confident readers to read out the listeners' questions. Encourage them to provide detailed answers when they are given the microphone.

Suggestion(s) for support

Let less confident children work with a partner to produce a combined contribution for the garden in Session One. During the radio programme in Session Two, direct the more straightforward questions at the less confident children to provide differentiation.

Assessment opportunities

Note the children's ability to speak confidently and appropriately when in role. Note any children who have difficulty in extending their answers when asked to provide more information for the imaginary listeners.

Opportunities for IT

Let two children act as sound technicians during the radio programme, using a cassette player to record the programme. The microphone should be placed near the presenter so that the questions are audible. As some of the answers may not be recorded clearly, it is best to repeat or summarize the children's answers in your role as radio presenter. The children will enjoy listening to the programme afterwards, either as a class or in small groups.

Children could use an art package to plan the princess's garden. They will need to know how to draw regular shapes such as squares, rectangles and circles; select different colours for the flowers, possibly using a spray tool to give the impression of flowers. They could plan the garden as an aerial view showing where the lawns, flowerbeds and other features are to go.

The children could extend this work using a word processor to write about the garden, giving instructions to the gardeners or listing the flowers that they are going to plant.

Display ideas

Let the children make a table top model of the garden, using clay, tissue paper or other suitable materials. Display this along with the wall plan of the garden.

Reference to photocopiable sheet

Photocopiable page 127 provides the listeners' questions about the plans for Snow White's garden. These are intended for use during the radio programme in Session Two.

Radio Palace: listeners' letters

Dear Radio Palace,
I would like to ask the planners what flowers they have put in Snow White's garden.
From Robert Green

Dear Radio Palace,
I would like to know if there is anywhere in the garden for Snow White to find shade from the sun on a hot day. Thank you.
From Kerry Harris

Dear Radio Palace,
Please could your special guests tell me where Snow White will be able to sit in the garden and if there is anywhere she could have a picnic. Thank you.
From Mr Charles Jackman

Dear Radio Palace,
Please would you ask the planners if they have put any buildings in Snow White's garden and if so, what are they for.
From Mrs Doris Shaw

Dear Radio Palace,
I have seen the gardeners working in the garden and they say it's the best garden they have ever made. Please would you ask the planners what are their favourite parts of the garden and why? Thank you.
From Aqueel Hassani

Dear Radio Palace,
If Snow White has any children to stay in her palace, will there be anywhere for them to play in the garden? Please will you ask the planners. Thank you.
From Benjamin Wood

Dear Radio Palace,
If Snow White and the Prince are in the garden and it starts to rain, will there be anywhere for them to shelter? Please will you ask your special guests. Thank you.
From Mrs White

I DON'T KNOW HOW TO

To use detailed mime to illustrate instructions.

Whole class.

15 minutes.

Previous skills/knowledge needed
The children should have some experience of baking. They should know how to dress themselves and how to get changed for PE.

Key background information
This activity focuses on a puppet who wants clear instructions on how to do things such as baking and changing for PE at school. These tasks have been selected as examples, but other tasks can be substituted if preferred. The activity seeks to motivate children to give detailed instructions by putting them in the position of experts who are there to help the puppet. The puppet needs the children to illustrate their instructions with mime. This introduces them to the link between words and movement and requires them to think carefully about the instructions in order to convey the meaning accurately in mime.

Preparation
Put the puppet in a box and place this wherever you plan to do the activity. If you are using the classroom, you will need to clear a large space for the children to sit in a circle. Make copies of photocopiable page [11] for the more confident children (optional).

Resources needed
Photocopiable page [11] (see above), a large space, a glove puppet that can express emotions of happiness and sadness.

What to do
Sit the children in a circle and bring out the puppet. Make it look sad and shy. Make it

communicate by whispering to you, so that you can pass on what it says to the children. Reveal that the puppet is sad because it will soon be going to school and is particularly worried about some of the activities. These activities are baking and getting changed for PE.

Now ask if the children will help the puppet by telling it how they do baking at school. Encourage them to talk about something they have all baked, such as buns or biscuits. After the children have explained how to bake the item, keep the puppet looking sad. Reveal that the puppet is sad because it can't understand everything the children have said. Suggest that they mime the actions to help the puppet understand. Say that it would help the puppet if they went through the instructions slowly and mimed them together.

Ask the children to give the first instruction for baking. Then ask everyone to mime this as you repeat the instruction out loud. Move on to the next instruction and let the children mime this in the same way. Encourage them to give step-by-step instructions. Repeat the procedure until the baking instructions are complete. If the children rush a particular mime, the puppet can ask them to repeat it more

DRAMA

slowly. Convey the puppet's thanks to the children and make it look a little happier for this advice. Finally, make the puppet ask about changing for PE. This time, let the children mime each instruction as they suggest it. End with the puppet looking very happy and waving goodbye before going back in the box.

Suggestion(s) for extension

Encourage more able children to give precise instructions and make their mimes very clear for the puppet. Extend the lesson by asking these children to try out the mimes on photocopiable page 128.

Suggestion(s) for support

This is a whole-group activity and differentiation is largely by outcome. Less confident children will tend to copy the other children if they are unsure. Direct suitable questions to these children when talking about the instructions, such as *Can you pretend to take off your shoes for PE, to show the puppet what to do?*

Assessment opportunities

Note those children who listen to the instructions and mime them appropriately with care. Look for children who can divide an activity into simple steps for mime.

Opportunities for IT

The children could use a word processor to help them write a list of instructions for other activities. They should be shown how to use the editing keys and how to move their instructions around to get them into the correct order.

Younger children could use framework software such as *My World*, or a word processor with a word bank or a concept keyboard to help them with the task. The teacher could prepare the software with a list of the instructions so that children simply have to select those which are appropriate and make sure they are in the correct order.

Display ideas

Make and display a class booklet entitled 'How to do it'. Include in this the children's sequenced pictures and sentences describing simple school activities for the puppet.

Reference to photocopiable sheet

Photocopiable page 128 provides an extension activity for more confident children. It requires them to break up three familiar activities into smaller actions and to then mime the activities. This exercise also encourages the general skill of breaking up an activity into its constituent parts when miming it.

THE LOST DOG

To build confidence in paired improvisation.

†† *Whole class and pairs.*

🕐 *30 to 45 minutes.*

Previous skills/knowledge needed

It would be helpful if the children had some previous knowledge about reporting lost items to the police.

Key background information

This activity builds children's confidence in improvised pair work by structuring the content of the improvisation beforehand. The context of a telephone conversation allows the children to concentrate on the language used in the improvisation.

Preparation

Prepare one copy per child of photocopiable page 129.

Resources needed

Photocopiable page 129, writing and drawing materials, a chalkboard or flip chart.

What to do

Introduction: Inventing the dogs

Ask the children to pretend that they have lost a pet dog. Talk generally about how and where dogs can get lost. Then organize the class into pairs to discuss how and where the children lost their own dogs. Give out copies of photocopiable page 129, and ask the children to draw a coloured picture of their dog and invent some details about it. Encourage them to discuss their work to ensure that each child has a different dog from their partner. Wait until most children have finished before moving on to the next part of the lesson.

Development: Role-play

Ask the children to pretend to telephone the police station to report their lost dogs. Explain that this kind of call would not be classed as a 999 emergency. Write the number of an imaginary local police station on the board for the children to use. Say that you are going to pretend to be the police officer on duty at the police station and will answer the phone when some of them call about their dogs.

Begin by asking the children what you should say when you first answer a call. Write this sentence on the board. Decide what questions you will ask about the lost dog and write these on the board in simple sentences. Then let one

or two individual children pretend to phone you up to report their lost dog. Write simple versions of their replies to your questions on the board.

Now ask each pair to conduct a similar conversation, taking turns at being the police officer and the person with the lost dog. Ask the children to add anything that might make their conversations sound more realistic. They can use the board and the questions on the photocopiable sheet

to help them if they wish. Remind the 'callers' that the role play is a telephone conversation and so they cannot show the police officer the pictures of their dogs. Help them avoid the temptation by making each pair sit back to back.

Give the children a minute to decide which part they will play first and to think about what they will say. Make sure everyone is ready to start at the same time, then begin. Keep an eye on the proceedings during the activity and make sure no-one stays in the same role for too long. If some pairs finish well before the others, let them swap pictures with other pairs and repeat the exercise using different dogs.

33

DRAMA

Conclusion

When most children have made an attempt at both roles, choose one or two pairs to perform their conversations to the class. Follow this with a brief discussion looking at how realistic the conversations were and how they could be made more convincing if necessary.

Suggestion(s) for extension

Extend the exercise by asking pairs to report the loss of other valuable items such as a watch, a bike, a camera, a bag or a purse. The more confident children may feel able to start their improvisations without the need to draw the missing items beforehand.

Suggestion(s) for support

At the start of the activity, differentiate through questioning when less confident children are selected to phone the police officer in front of the whole class. Use 'either/or' type questions, such as: *Is your dog a big dog or a small dog?* During the role-play exercise, let less confident pairs act out a conversation at the police station instead of a telephone conversation. This will allow them to use their

pictures if they wish. Encourage them to concentrate on telling the police where and how they lost the dog.

Assessment opportunities

Assess the children's ability to speak confidently and clearly when working in role with a partner. Note any children who are able to extend the improvisation appropriately, within the context of the given situation.

The children could use an art or drawing package to design their own poster offering a reward for the lost dog. They could use pictures taken form a clip art collection or scanned from their own line drawings or photographs of their own pets, or do drawings using the art package.

Older or more able children could write a short advert to go into the classified section of the local paper or local shop. They could work to a limited word count, maybe 20 words and use the word processor to write and then edit their advert. If the word processor has a word count facility this could be used to check on the number of words used. The adverts could be collected together and put into a simple desktop publishing package to create a 'classified ads' section of a class newspaper.

Opportunities for IT

The children could use an art or drawing package to design their own poster offering a reward for the lost dog. They could use pictures taken from a clip art collection or scanned from their own line drawings, photographs of their own pets or drawn using an art package.

Older or more able children could write a short advert to go into the classified section of the local paper or local shop. They could work to a limited word count, maybe 20 words and use the word processor to write and then edit their advert. If the word processor has a word count facility this could be used to check on the number of words used. The adverts could be collected together and put into a simple desktop publishing package to create a 'classified ads' section of a class newspaper.

Performance ideas

Some children may like to rehearse and then record their telephone conversations onto an audio cassette, to be played to the class.

Display ideas

Let the children make 'reward' posters for their lost dogs and use these to create a simple but colourful display.

Reference to photocopiable sheet

Photocopiable page 129 can be used to help the children invent and discuss details of their lost dogs, so that they are well prepared for the improvisations during the role-play exercise.

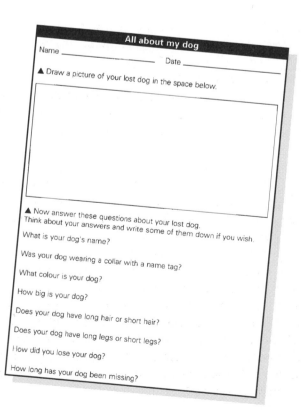

All about my dog

Name _____ Date _____

▲ Draw a picture of your lost dog in the space below.

▲ Now answer these questions about your lost dog. Think about your answers and write some of them down if you wish.

What is your dog's name?

Was your dog wearing a collar with a name tag?

What colour is your dog?

How big is your dog?

Does your dog have long hair or short hair?

Does your dog have long legs or short legs?

How did you lose your dog?

How long has your dog been missing?

LOOKING FOR SITA

To act out parts of a story through dance drama.
†† *Whole class.*
🕐 *30 to 45 minutes.*

Previous skills/knowledge needed

The children should be familiar with the story of 'Rama and Sita' (see *Festivals*, *Teacher Timesavers* series, Scholastic; *Stories from the Hindu World*, by Jamila Gavin, Macdonald). They should have some basic experience in movement and dance and be able to start and stop their movements on a given signal. ('The clockmaker's dream' on page 19 gives practice in stopping and starting on the beat of a tambour.)

Key background information

This activity relates to the Hindu Diwali Festival and the story of Rama and Sita. In the story Prince Rama, his wife Princess Sita and his brother are in exile in a forest. One day, a demon king called Ravana disguises himself as a holy man and steals Sita away. Rama and his brother search through the forest for Sita, until they reach the mountain kingdom of the Ape King, who helps Rama locate where Sita is being held prisoner. After battles led by the Ape King and other attempts to rescue Sita, Rama finally comes face to face with Ravana and kills him. This ends Rama and Sita's exile and they are eventually crowned king and queen of their kingdom.

In dance drama, the narrative of the drama is expressed through movement rather than words. The dance drama in this activity focuses on the first part of the story, where Rama discovers that Sita has been captured by Ravana and travels through the forest to reach the mountain kingdom of the Ape King.

DRAMA

when you shake the tambourine, they must slowly stand up and make their whole body look angry, just like Rama. Encourage them to do this by making their arms, legs, hands and head look strong. They should hold this position on the beat of the tambour to make an angry statue. Make it clear that from this point on in the lesson, all movements must start and stop on the beat of the tambour.

The drama: Rama is angry

Ask the children to bring their statues to life and make angry movements on the spot, such as stamping their feet and shaking their fists. Now ask them to lift one foot high to stamp down hard on the floor. Emphasize that just before their foot hits the floor, however, they should slow the movement down to put their foot down gently. Ask them to use this technique to stamp around the hall or classroom with soft-sounding steps.

Next, ask the children to make two stamps followed by a leap into the air with waving arms and clenched fists, finishing on a freeze. Encourage them to leap as high as they can, with an angry face and body. Remind them to stretch their arms and make strong movements. Then ask them to repeat this sequence (stamp/ stamp/ leap/ freeze) several times as they travel around the room. Keep this activity quite short and stress the need to move into spaces and be aware of others. Finish by asking the children to make their angry statues once more. Then, using the tambourine to accompany them, let the statues turn slowly back into clay.

Now repeat the movements into the following order again, using the tambour to start and stop the action: *grow into a statue of the angry Rama / stamp and leap as the statue comes to life / turn back into an angry statue / melt into clay.*

Journey through the forest

Talk about how Rama searched hard for Sita, travelling quickly but quietly through the forest, ever fearful of the demon Ravana's tricks. Then ask the children to find a space. Encourage them to move around the room as if they were Rama travelling through the forest, listening and watching for danger. Suggest that they step over tree roots and duck under low branches as they walk. Now ask half the children to stand as if they were trees with low branches. Let the other half of the class move around the trees and under the branches. Then repeat with the children exchanging

Preparation

Read the story of Rama and Sita to the children. Focus particularly on the events in the first part as these form the basis of the activity below. Make sure the children are dressed in a PE kit or similar suitable clothing.

Resources needed

A large space, a tambourine, a tambour.

What to do

Introduction

Sit the whole class together. Discuss briefly what makes people angry. Talk about how angry Rama must have been when he discovered that Ravana the demon had taken his wife Sita. Ask the children to make an angry face when you bang the tambour. Repeat this and ask the children to look at each other to see how their faces change.

Now ask them to find a space and sit down. Explain that

roles. Suggest that Rama may have had to leap over stepping stones to cross streams and let the children imitate this action.

Now organize the movements into the following sequence, again using the tambour to start and stop the action:

travel through the forest (under and around trees) / leap over stepping stones / stop to listen and watch.

Reaching the mountain kingdom

Remind the children that Rama finally reached the mountain kingdom of the Ape King, who believed he knew where to find Sita. Ask them to make a mountain with their bodies to finish the dance drama. To do this, the children should stand with their legs apart. They then place their hands above their heads with palms together, to make the shape of a mountain top. Now tell them to make themselves higher by balancing on the balls of their feet. Let them hold this for a few seconds before trying again.

Conclusion: The story in sequence

Now repeat all the sequences practised above to tell the story, signalling when to stop and start with the tambour. The order should be as follows:

grow into an angry statue of Rama / stamp twice, leap with clenched fists, then freeze / make an angry statue again / melt back into clay / travel through the forest, stepping under and around trees / leap over a stream using stepping stones / stop to listen and watch / make the shape of a mountain / relax.

Suggestion(s) for extension

Incorporate some of the children's own ideas into the forest journey sequence. Let the more able children work in pairs to create their own sequence of travelling movements. Extend the activity by asking pairs of children to work out a simple sequence to represent climbing up the mountain.

Suggestion(s) for support

Pair up less confident children with those who will support them. Ask these pairs to work together as Rama and his brother who travelled together to search for Sita.

Assessment opportunities

Note the children's ability to share the space with others and use the space well as they move. Note also their ability to respond to stopping and starting signals. Look for imaginative and expressive interpretations of the movements.

Performance ideas

Let the children rehearse and perform their dance drama to an audience. When performing the forest journey section, let a group of children represent the trees, as in the lesson. Give all the children the opportunity to perform the angry sequence and to make the final mountain position.

THE PIED PIPER

To use whole-group drama to act out a well-known story.

♦♦ *Whole class and groups.*

🕐 *Session One: 45 minutes. Session Two: 30 minutes.*

Previous skills/knowledge needed

The children should be familiar with the story of the Pied Piper. It would also be helpful to have some experience of starting and stopping on a given signal (see 'Looking for Sita' on page 35).

Key background information

This activity will help the children become familiar with the sequence of events and the feelings of some of the characters in the Pied Piper story. As they act out the various parts, they see events from the perspective of the Hamelin villagers, engaging them in a personal relationship with the story. The drama is split into two sessions which should be separated by no more than a week. Both sessions require a large space, but the conclusion to the first session can take place in the classroom.

Preparation

Make one copy per child of photocopiable page 130. For Session One, space six chairs evenly around three walls surrounding a large acting space. For Session Two, make a short cassette tape of a child or adult playing a simple recorder tune and set this up ready to play. Arrange the acting space as before, but make a gap between the wall and each chair, so that you can walk behind each chair.

Resources needed

Photocopiable page 130, a large space, writing materials, six chairs, a whistle, a cloak (to represent both the mayor and the Pied Piper), a cassette player, taped recorder music (see above).

What to do
Session One

Organize the children into six groups and number them one to six. Put children into pairs or threes within each group. Ask them if they will pretend to be the villagers of Hamelin in the story of the Pied Piper. First, talk briefly about what village life would have been like in the time the story is set, compared to today. Then allocate one chair to each group and ask the children to imagine that the spaces in front of the chairs are houses in Hamelin. Explain that, during the activity, they will need to mime anything they use and talk as if they were the villagers from long ago.

Ask each group to sit on the floor in front of their chair and turn to face you. Explain that they will be acting out parts of the Pied Piper story, starting with exploring what village life might have been like before the rats arrived.

Explain that the drama will start on an ordinary day, when the people are working on simple jobs in their houses and gardens. These jobs could include washing clothes, planting vegetables, cleaning, baking, building walls and so on. Then ask each pair or group of three to decide on what they will be doing on that particular day. They should fold their arms when they have decided.

Scene 1: Before the rats arrive Explain that when you say 'Action', the whole village should come alive and go about their chosen jobs. Tell them they should stop immediately when you blow the whistle and say 'Freeze'. Start the children off, then after a minute or two tell the children to return to sit in front of their chairs. Now let groups one to three perform their version of daily village life to the other half of the class, then let groups four to six do the same.

Scene 2: The rats invade Explain that you will now be moving time on to when the rats arrived in the villagers' houses. Ask the children to think about how the villagers might have tried to rid themselves of the rats, such as using traps, poison or chasing them with sticks. Then give each pair a few minutes to decide on two ways they will use to try to get the rats out of their house. Explain that, eventually, the villagers became so used to the rats that they didn't scream or run away any more when they saw them. Warn that any silly or noisy reactions, therefore, will be unacceptable. Now bring the village to life again as the villagers try to get rid of the rats.

Scene 3: Bad rats! Remind the children of the Pied Piper story and talk about some of the bad things the rats did in the village, such as biting babies in their cradles, eating

soup from the ladles, making too much noise, and so on. Ask each pair to make up something bad that happened to them involving a rat and tell them to fold their arms when they have finished. Now give them a short time to act out their scenario before stopping the drama again.

Scene 4: Meeting the mayor
Stand at the side of the acting space where there are no chairs and call the children to sit in front of you. Ask them to imagine that this is the entrance to the town hall of Hamelin and that they have come to see the mayor. Explain that they need to tell the mayor how bad the rats are and then request his help. Tell them that when you put on the cloak, you will play the part of the mayor. Ask

for a volunteer to be the first to speak to the Mayor and let the class decide on what that child should say. Make it clear that after this child has spoken, any of the other villagers can speak. If you have a large class, suggest that they put their hands up before speaking to the mayor.

Now start the drama again by putting on the cloak and asking the villagers what they want. Plead ignorance about the extent of the problem and ask the villagers to give you examples of what things the rats have done. Demand to know what measures they have already taken to solve the problem before finally agreeing to offer a reward to anyone who can rid Hamelin of rats. Take off the cloak to come out of role.

Conclude this part of the drama by giving each child one copy of photocopiable page 130 to complete with the help of their partner. Read through the sheet with the whole class first, and then explain that they will act out the rest of the story in the next drama lesson.

The photocopiable sheet should be used by the children to recap on the sequence of events in the story when they come to do Session Two.

Session Two
Scene 5: The Pied Piper arrives Explain that the drama will begin as the Pied Piper comes round each house to tempt the rats to follow him to the river, where they will drown. Choose a child to wear the cloak and play the Pied Piper or play the part yourself. Next, explain the following procedure to the class. Each group must sit in front of their chair and wait for the Pied Piper to walk behind the chair as though walking behind their house. When the Pied Piper visits, they should stand up and open all the cupboards and

containers to let the rats escape. The Pied Piper will then move on to visit each of the other five houses. Each group should sit back down after the Pied Piper has left their house.

Explain that the Pied Piper will pretend to play the pipe as the tape plays. After visiting the last house, the Pied Piper should walk a short way as if taking the rats to the river. When you stop the tape, everyone should shout 'Hurrah, the rats are dead!'. After explaining this and making sure the children understand what to do, perform this sequence as described and rewind the tape afterwards.

Scene 6: The Pied Piper's revenge Tell the children that you are now moving time on to when the Pied Piper became angry because the Mayor refused to pay him and decided to lead the children of Hamelin away. Ask the children if they will now play the parts of the children of Hamelin. Explain that this will be acted out in a similar way to when the rats were led away, but this time, the groups will pretend to be the children playing in their gardens as the Pied Piper comes by.

Give each pair of children a few minutes to decide what game they will play, for example playing ball or skipping. Then explain that as the Pied Piper passes the back of their house and plays his music, they should follow him in a line. After visiting each house to collect the children, the Pied Piper will lead the children to dance around the room before taking them to the mountain at the opposite end. When the tape stops and you say 'Freeze', the children should stand still in a silent depiction of the moment when they become trapped inside the mountain. Check that everyone is clear about what to do, then perform the sequence as described.

DRAMA

imaginatively as villagers and note those who are confident when talking in a whole-group role-play situation such as at the meeting with the mayor.

Opportunities for IT
The children could use a word processor to write captions for their pictures telling the story of the Pied Piper. They could also use it to write speech bubbles to cut out and add to the display. The children may need to experiment with the font size to make sure their captions and speech bubbles are large enough to be read from a display.

Performance ideas
Adapt the scenes involving the Pied Piper (Session Two) for a smaller space and polish them up to make a performance for a wider audience.

Display ideas
Let the children draw themselves as village children. Use their pictures to create a frieze of the children being led away by the Pied Piper. Let the children write in some thought bubbles for a few children and also for the Pied Piper.

Reference to photocopiable sheet
Photocopiable page 130 will help the children to remember the sequence of events in the whole story. This can be used to prepare them for acting out the final part of the story in Session Two.

Afterwards, sit everyone together and ask them to describe what they were thinking and feeling when they realized they were trapped inside the mountain. Who did they think was to blame for what happened to the children of Hamelin? Was it the mayor or the Pied Piper, or both? Did the Pied Piper have a right to be angry? Should he have taken revenge in this way? Encourage the children to give reasons for their answers.

Suggestion(s) for extension
During Session One, ask more confident children to act out a conversation between the villagers about how the rats are affecting their lives. Let them perform this spontaneously to the rest of the class before the children meet the mayor. Choose two confident children to play the part of the Pied Piper each time in Session Two.

Suggestion(s) for support
Put less confident children in a mixed-ability group of three for both sessions. If necessary, support them by joining in as one of the villagers when you can.

Assessment opportunities
Look for children who respond appropriately and

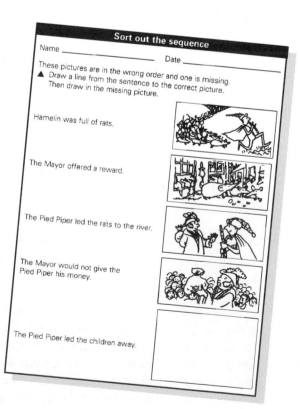

DRAMA

Acting for an audience

Many children enjoy performing to an audience and should be given the opportunity to develop their confidence and skills in this area. This is particularly important for those who are unable to succeed in other curriculum areas. Acting for an audience can help to increase children's confidence and self esteem. However, some children find performing in front of others difficult and forcing them to do this should certainly be avoided. Give less confident children plenty of opportunities to take part in performances at whatever level they feel comfortable with, until they are ready to take a more active part.

The activities in this chapter are presented in a non-threatening way, allowing children to make their own choices about what they will do and say when acting in front of others. Some children will choose to extend and develop their improvisations, while others will be content to make a minimal contribution. However, all children need time to think about and try out what they will be asked to perform. The activities here are structured to allow them to do this.

In this chapter, the children are introduced to the idea of using objects and pictures to stimulate playmaking and are given opportunities to act in large groups and in pairs. Some of the lessons also focus on particular acting skills, such as mime and movement. There are exercises to build confidence in manipulating simple puppets and talking in different voices. These are designed to increase children's awareness of acting skills in an enjoyable way. Advice on rehearsing children for a school play and ideas for preparing children for a theatre visit are also included.

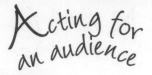

WALKING ALL AROUND

To develop skills in using movement and expression in role.

Whole class and small groups.

20 to 30 minutes.

Previous skills/knowledge needed
Children need to be familiar with the terms 'Action' and 'Freeze' for stopping and starting a movement activity (see 'Sequencing a story' on page 21).

Key background information
This activity will help the children to see how movement is affected by situation and emotion. The movement implications of a particular situation or emotion should always be discussed before the children attempt each activity. Point up good practice when the children perform to each other, for example the use of appropriate and expressive movements and convincing facial expressions. Use the words 'Action' and 'Freeze' to start and stop the movements each time.

Preparation
Fill the box with the everyday objects (see below) and put it to one side until needed.

Resources needed
A large space, one everyday object per child (for example newspapers, comics, aprons, hats, sweeping brushes, dusters, toys, walking sticks) and a box large enough to contain them.

What to do
Introduction: Walking in different environments
Start by asking the children to walk around the hall as if they are on their own. Next, ask them to think about how they might move if they were walking in deep snow. Invite some of them to demonstrate this. Talk about how the snow forces us to walk slowly and pick our feet up higher than normal. Now let everyone try walking around as if in deep snow. Extend this to walking through other environments such as splashing through puddles, paddling in the sea, walking through long grass, walking over a wobbly bridge or walking on an icy path.

Development: Walking with feelings
Now ask the children to walk as if they are feeling very happy. Talk about how this will affect their movement and facial expressions before they start. Then stop the class and ask the children to repeat their happy walking, but this time they should shake hands with others they meet on the way. Invite two children to demonstrate shaking hands in a friendly, happy way before letting the others start.

Next, split the class into two and let each half take it in turn to perform their happy walks. Then repeat the sequence using other emotions, such as sadness, anger, fear, excitement, tiredness and boredom. Now link a situation and an emotion by asking the children to walk as

if they are feeling: (a) worried because they are late for school; (b) happy because they have won a prize; (c) bored, shopping for food with a grown up; (d) very cold, paddling in the sea; (e) very angry because someone has broken their favourite toy. In each case, remember to discuss briefly how these situations and emotions will affect the children's movement and expressions before they start.

Using an object
Organize the class into small groups and give each child an everyday object from the box (see 'Preparation'). Tell them to look at their object carefully and to think of who might own or use it. Explain that they are going to pretend to be this person using the object. Give them a few minutes to discuss in their groups how they will use their objects and what kind of people they might be. Then ask a few volunteers to each demonstrate their ideas to the class.

Now let everyone move around the room pretending to be someone using their particular object. Stop the activity and ask the children to put down the items and fold their arms. Then invite each group to perform to the class. After each performance, ask the audience questions about who the people might be and draw attention to the way they moved when using the objects. Finish by asking each child to put their object back in the box as if they were the person who owned it.

Conclusion: Reflection
Hold a brief discussion by asking the children to reflect on the different emotions conveyed and how these feelings affected the way they moved in each case.

Suggestion(s) for extension
Extend the 'Walking in different environments' section by asking the more confident children to demonstrate moving like particular characters in different circumstances, such as walking like an elderly person with a stick, a parent with a pushchair, a gardener with a wheel barrow or a person being pulled by a large dog.

Suggestion(s) for support
This is largely a whole-group activity with differentiation by outcome. However, it may help to support less able children by pairing them with more confident children, especially when using the objects. You can also join in the activities yourself to support these children where necessary.

Assessment opportunities
Note how well the children use their bodies and facial expressions to convey the situations and emotions. Note also how confident the children are when performing.

Opportunities for IT
The children could use an art package to create their own faces to depict different emotions. These could be cut out and made into a class display. Some specific software like

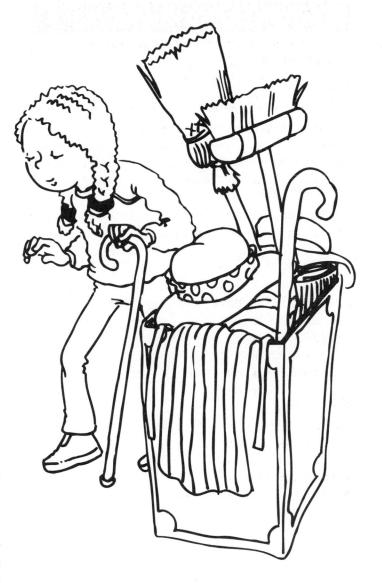

Smart Alex from Brilliant Computing enables children to create faces from a range of different parts and explore and develop vocabulary around them.

If the school has access to a digital camera the teacher or children could take pictures during the activity. They could even take pictures trying to show them expressing other emotions. The pictures could be saved onto the computer and used in word processed work based on the activity.

Performance ideas
Ask pairs of children to practise walking as if they are feeling these emotions and let them take turns to perform one emotion each from the list.

Display ideas
Put up a list of the emotions covered in the drama. Ask the children to draw faces expressing these emotions on paper plates to make a display.

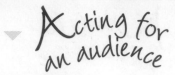

LET'S MIME IT!

To develop confidence in the use of mime by performing simple activities.

†† *Whole class and pairs.*

🕐 *30 to 45 minutes.*

Previous skills/knowledge needed

The children should know the words to the song 'Here we go round the mulberry bush'. They should have experience in playing with a ball, bat and skipping rope, and have a basic idea of how to build a garden fence and plant flowers.

Key background information

It is often inappropriate to comment on the accuracy of children's mime during an ongoing role-play activity, as this can interrupt the narrative and destroy belief in the drama. This activity provides an opportunity to focus on mime for its own sake, with the express purpose of building children's confidence and skill. The children should be encouraged to carry out these activities with as much care and precision as possible within the limits of their concentration. Throughout the activity, stress the need to exaggerate movements to make the mimes clear.

Preparation

Make one copy of photocopiable page 131.

Resources needed

Photocopiable page 131, a room with enough space for the children to stand in a large circle and, if necessary for reference, a copy of 'Here we go round the mulberry bush' in *Oranges and Lemons* by Ian Beck and Karen King (Oxford).

What to do

Stand the children in a large circle, with plenty of space between each child. Sing and dance 'Here we go round the mulberry bush' including actions for getting up in the morning, such as cleaning teeth, washing, brushing hair

and getting dressed. Then repeat these actions without the song to include more detailed mime. For example, cleaning teeth would involve picking up the toothbrush, picking up the toothpaste and putting it on the brush, putting the toothpaste back, turning on the tap, cleaning the teeth properly and rinsing the mouth.

Now ask the children to imagine that they each have a large ball to play with. Tell them to throw the ball up in the air and catch it. Encourage them to follow the ball with their eyes as it moves. Extend this activity to bouncing the ball and then throwing and catching it in pairs. Move on to

carefully bouncing a small imaginary ball on a bat and then playing bat and ball with a partner. Now ask the children to skip on the spot with imaginary skipping ropes. Finish the skipping by asking them to fold up their ropes and sit down.

Read aloud the story on photocopiable sheet 131 and help the children to decide on some appropriate mimes for building the fence and planting the flowers. Then read the story again, this time with the children miming the actions in the appropriate places. Explain that they must listen carefully to the story to know when to start and end their mimes, as you will not be using any signal to tell them.

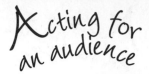
Suggestion(s) for extension

Give confident children more complicated activities to mime, such as washing dishes, washing a dog, painting a fence, wrapping a birthday present or making a sandwich.

Suggestion(s) for support

Prepare less confident children for the more detailed mimes by incorporating these actions into the 'Here we go round the mulberry bush' song. For example: *'This is the way we... throw a ball... bounce a ball... bat a ball... skip with a rope... build a fence... plant some flowers'*.

Assessment opportunities

Look out for those children who concentrate well on the mime tasks and are able to pay some attention to accuracy.

Display ideas

The children can paint or draw pictures of the garden described in the story for display. Their pictures can show what the garden looks like when the sun is shining and when it is raining.

Performance ideas

Let pairs of children use photocopiable page 131 to learn and perform the mimes in the story as a sequence of events.

Reference to photocopiable sheet

Photocopiable page 131 provides a structure for miming simple actions in the context of a story about a garden.

DIFFERENT VOICES

To build confidence in speaking in a different voice in front of the class.

👫 *Whole class and pairs.*

🕐 *15 to 20 minutes.*

Previous skills/knowledge

None are necessary, apart from feeling secure enough to speak out in front of the whole class.

Key background information

Most children enjoy the opportunity to experiment with their voices and explore the different effects they can achieve. This activity is intended to be fun as well as building confidence in speaking in a different voice. However, it is important to focus the children's attention on speaking clearly in whatever voice they are using.

Preparation

Clear a small space at the front of the classroom.

Resources needed

A small space, a chalkboard or flip chart.

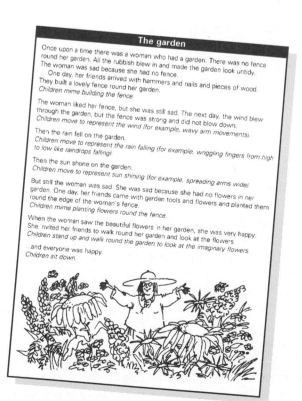

The garden

Once upon a time there was a woman who had a garden. There was no fence round her garden. All the rubbish blew in and made the garden look untidy. The woman was sad because she had no fence.
One day, her friends arrived with hammers and nails and pieces of wood. They built a lovely fence round her garden.
Children mime building the fence.

The woman liked her fence, but she was still sad. The next day, the wind blew through the garden, but the fence was strong and did not blow down.
Children move to represent the wind (for example, wavy arm movements).

Then the rain fell on the garden.
Children move to represent the rain falling (for example, wriggling fingers from high to low like raindrops falling).

Then the sun shone on the garden.
Children move to represent sun shining (for example, spreading arms wide).

But still the woman was sad. She was sad because she had no flowers in her garden. One day, her friends came with garden tools and flowers and planted them round the edge of the woman's fence.
Children mime planting flowers round the fence.

When the woman saw the beautiful flowers in her garden, she was very happy. She invited her friends to walk round her garden and look at the flowers.
Children stand up and walk round the garden to look at the imaginary flowers.

...and everyone was happy.
Children sit down.

What to do

Tell the class that you are going to say your name using a different voice from normal. Do this, then repeat it using another voice. Now let the children practise saying their own names in a different voice, but stress that they should still speak clearly. Now invite each child to say their name to the class using their different voice.

Next, explain that you will ask each child a simple question, but whatever the question, they must answer it by saying 'Bananas' in a different voice, without laughing. Demonstrate this by questioning a few of the more confident children first, then ask everyone else a question in turn. Make sure that the 'Bananas' answer will be amusing by asking questions such as: *What do you wear to bed? What do you eat with gravy? What do you like to read? What do you paint with at school?*, and so on.

Now write the words 'Hello my friend' on the board and ask the children to read it aloud with you. Tell them that you are going to say these words in a deep voice. Demonstrate this and then let the children copy you. Repeat this using a squeaky voice, a loud voice and a quiet voice.

Finally, ask one of the children to stand at the front with their back to the class. Then silently point to one of the class and ask them to say the words 'Hello my friend' in a different voice. They should say this phrase twice so that the words are clear. The child at the front then turns round

and has two guesses to point to the person who spoke. Repeat the activity, letting the children take turns to come to the front.

Suggestion(s) for extension

Let confident children ask some of the questions in the 'Bananas' activity. They can also say a few lines from a nursery rhyme in a different voice, instead of the phrase 'Hello my friend'. Conclude the activity by letting these children record themselves reciting rhymes in different voices onto an audio tape. Encourage them to check their recording for clarity and re-record if necessary.

Suggestion(s) for support

If some children are reluctant to say their names in a different voice, let them choose another child to say it for them. Give them the option to say 'Bananas' in their own voice first and then invite them to repeat the word in a different voice if they wish. If they prefer, they can say 'Bananas' instead of 'Hello my friend' in the final part of the activity.

Assessment opportunities

This activity provides a good opportunity to assess children's confidence in speaking in front of a group, as well as their ability to speak clearly and use their voices imaginatively.

Opportunities for IT

The children could record some of their different voices using a tape recorder. An alternative activity would be for the children to use specific software and a microphone to record their own voices onto the computer.

The recorded voices could be used in a simple multimedia presentation using authoring software. These could be linked to a picture or sentence with an option of three or four different children saying or describing the same thing. Clicking on a child's name displayed on the page would play the recorded voice of that child. An alternative strategy would be to set up the software to enable the user to try and guess from a list of three or four names, who had said the word or sentence.

Obviously such activities are fairly sophisticated and the teacher would need to set up the pages and framework in advance. Extra help for the children would also be needed if they were to create the pages for themselves.

Performance ideas

Encourage them to use different voice levels, such as deep, squeaky, loud and quiet. They can then perform these to the rest of the class.

Display ideas

Display a variety of short sentences, rhymes or jokes. Let the children practise reading these clearly using different voices.

Who is speaking?

"Hello my friend"

Is it

➢John   ➢Resham

➢Balpinder   ➢Elizabeth

Click a name
to see if you are right

Answer
Well done!
Yes it was Resham

A DAY OUT

To move from structured dramatic play to performance.

†† *Whole class and small groups.*

🕐 *45 minutes.*

Previous skills/knowledge needed

It would be helpful if the children had discussed beforehand some possible activities for days out on the beach and at the park.

Key background information

This activity is initially conducted as a role play by the whole class, without an audience. This allows the children to try out and extend their acting in a non-threatening situation before being asked to perform. Point out any examples of good practice after the group performances, rather than interrupting the spontaneous flow of the whole-group work. Using the suggested notices forbidding swimming should limit opportunities for boisterous behaviour.

DRAMA

Later in the activity, the children are asked to work in groups to make up their own play about a day out at the park. Groups are supported by suggestions from the class and prompts on the photocopiable sheet to help them structure and sequence their plays. Use the words 'Action' and 'Freeze' to start and stop the drama in this activity.

Preparation
Make two copies of photocopiable sheet 132 per group of three or four children. Let some children use a word processor to make two warning notices saying 'No swimming' or write them out yourself. Put these on the wall.

Resources
Photocopiable sheet 132, a word processor (optional), writing materials, two sheets of A4 paper, Blu-tack or adhesive tape, a large space.

What to do
Introduction
Sit the children in a large circle with plenty of space between

them. Say that you would like everyone to be in a play. Explain that the play will be about some children and their teacher who go for a day out to the beach. Talk about the things you might do on the beach. Refer to the notices which forbid swimming, but explain that it will be possible to paddle in the rock pools. Discuss a range of activities such as making sandcastles, paddling, collecting shells, fishing in pools, playing with beach toys and eating sandwiches and ice cream. Make suggestions yourself if necessary.

Development: Acting as a whole class
Explain that the beach activities will need to be mimed in the play, but the children will be allowed to speak. Let them practise the mimes for each activity. As they do this, invite them to suggest what they might talk about when they come to do the activities in the play. Ask them to decide what they will do first on the beach and agree on an order for the other activities.

Remind the children of the first activity and start the play. Act as if you were really there and encourage the dialogue by talking to individual children about what they are doing. Keep in role, but direct the progress by suggesting when it is time to move on to the next activity. After the final activity, suggest that everyone sits down for a rest and then stop the drama.

Now organize the children into small groups of three or four. Say that you would like them to show each other one or two of the things they did at the beach in the play. Give the groups a few minutes to practise at least two activities, then sit everyone in a large circle. Let two or three groups at a time perform their plays in the middle of the circle. Remind them that they can talk if they wish. After each performance, ask the class to identify the activities and pick out the things they liked best about the performance. Add comments yourself to point out good practice, such as careful and accurate mime or any attempts at appropriate dialogue.

Conclusion: A day at the park

Explain that the children are now going to work in their groups to create another play, this time about a day out at the park. Talk about some possible activities and discuss how these might be mimed. Then give out two copies of photocopiable page 132 per group. Explain that the pictures on the sheet will help them to make up their group play, together with their own ideas. Look at each activity on the sheet and discuss how it could be mimed. Then talk about possibilities for dialogue. Give the groups a few minutes to make up their plays. After a while, stop the work and tell them to have a final practice. Then let them perform their plays to each other, one group at a time. Remember to point out any good practice, as before.

Suggestion(s) for extension

Put the more confident children together in groups of three and encourage them to include plenty of appropriate dialogue when performing. Let them incorporate their own ideas into their play and/or extend those suggested on the photocopiable sheet.

Suggestion(s) for support

Work alongside those children who need support during the whole-group role-play and be prepared to perform their activities with them in the circle. Encourage less confident groups to focus on the photocopiable sheet to help them make a simple mime sequence of the day out.

Assessment opportunities

Look for children who are confident when acting in front of an audience. Note those who are confident in a whole-group situation, but are less so when confronted with an audience. Look for those children who can co-operate and negotiate when making up a play in a small group.

Performance ideas

The children's beach and park activities can be developed and performed as a dance drama on the theme of summer activities.

Display ideas

These activities can be recorded in pictures to create a display.

Reference to photocopiable sheet

Photocopiable page 132 provides suggestions and a possible structure for groups to make up their own play about a day at the park.

A day at the park
▲ Use these pictures to help you make up a play about a day at the park.

1. Playing ball on the grass.
2. Feeding the ducks.
3. Rowing a boat.
4. Playing on the swings.
5. Buying and eating an ice cream.
6. Looking at the flowers.

SHOPPING CENTRE

To give practice in paired improvisations and responding as an audience.

†† *Whole class and pairs.*

⏲ *Session One: 15 to 20 minutes. Session Two: 20 minutes.*

Previous skills/knowledge needed

Some discussion on the different types of shops in a shopping centre would be helpful prior to the drama. Children should be familiar with the words 'Action' and 'Freeze' as starting and stopping signals for drama.

Key background information

This activity gives children the opportunity to work in pairs to develop simple improvisations on a shopping theme. The situations are simple and tightly structured to help children gain confidence in working in this way. The children learn to work as actors and also have the opportunity to respond as an audience to each other's work. Session One

can be carried out in a classroom, but Session Two will require a larger space. The toy shop improvisation acts as an introduction to the greater demands of the shoe shop improvisation.

Preparation
Make one copy of photocopiable page 133 per child. Make a sign from A4 card saying 'Shoe Shop'.

Resources needed
Photocopiable page 133, writing materials, a sheet of A4 card, a chair, a large space (for Session Two).

What to do
Session One
Organize the children into pairs and sit them down. Give each child a copy of photocopiable page 133. Explain that they are going to act out being shop assistants and customers in a toy shop and a shoe shop, and this sheet will help them with ideas. Discuss possible actions when improvising a visit to a toy shop, such as paying for toys and putting them in a bag. Talk about how the shop assistants might greet the customers. Let some children demonstrate this, then read through the photocopiable sheet with the class and ask them to complete the Part A only. They should work in their pairs to help each other with this task.

As each pair complete their sheets, ask them to take turns to be the customer and shop assistant at the toy shop. Let some children perform their role plays to the class. Then talk about visiting a shoe shop. Discuss the difference between what happens in a toy shop and a shoe shop. Then ask the children to complete the Part B of the photocopiable sheet.

Session Two
Place the 'Shoe Shop' sign on the chair at one side of the room, in front of a space. Ask the children to pretend that the area in front of the chair is now a shoe shop. Remind them what happens in a shoe shop and talk about what the shop assistants and customers might say to each other. Demonstrate what is required by asking a child to be the customer while you play the shop assistant, or let two confident children perform this.

Now explain that each person must work with their partner in the shop and take it in turns to be the shop assistant and the customer as before. Tell those who will be the shop assistants first to stand in the designated shoe shop area. Give the customers a minute to think about the type of shoes they want before visiting the shop, and allow the shop assistants time to think about what they will say to the customers. Then send the customers to the shoe shop area to buy some new shoes from their partner. Tell the pairs to return to the side of the room and sit down when they have finished.

After the activity ask each pair to perform what happened to them in the shop. Let two pairs perform at a time if you have a large class. Ask the children watching to pick out the things they liked about the performances and to praise any interesting dialogue or events. Point out things such as shop assistants helping customers with laces or buckles or the customers asking for specific types of shoe. If these do not occur in the improvisations, then suggest that the children include them next time. Then ask the pairs to change roles and repeat the activity.

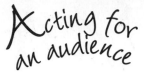
Suggestion(s) for extension

Put the more confident children together and after they have filled in their photocopiable sheet for Session One, ask them to work out a good role play of shopping in the toy shop to show the class. Ask them to include a conversation about why the customer is buying those particular toys. Encourage them to include as much relevant dialogue as possible.

Suggestion(s) for support

If some children cannot fill in their photocopiable sheet, let them draw a picture of the toys they intend to buy. In Session Two, they can draw the new shoes they will ask for in the shoe shop. Let them show these pictures to the shop assistant to explain what they want when playing the customer. Give them a simple phrase to use when they are playing the part of a shop assistant, for example: *'Yes please?'* or *'Can I help you?'*. Alternatively, join a pair of less confident children yourself to support or direct their activities.

Assessment opportunities

Look for children who can respond appropriately in role and speak confidently in front of an audience. Note any children who attempt to vary their vocabulary and tone of voice, to suit the role they are playing. Look for those who use extended dialogue appropriate to the situation.

Performance ideas

Let pairs of children use pictures of sweets and bread items to make up shopping improvisations to perform to the whole class.

Display ideas

Display these pictures in the windows of a baker's shop and a sweet shop.

Reference to photocopiable sheet

Photocopiable page 133 provides an introduction to both stages of the activity by focusing children's attention on what could be involved when improvising a visit to each shop.

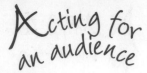

MOVING PICTURES

To develop freeze-frames into improvisations.

✝✝ *Small groups performing to the whole class.*

🕐 *30 to 45 minutes.*

Previous skills/knowledge needed

Children should have some experience of making freeze-frames (see 'Special moments' on page14 and should be able to work co-operatively in small groups.

Key background information

This activity uses the freeze-frame as a structure for small group improvisation. It uses a picture as a stimulus, so that the children can concentrate on the subsequent improvisation and concluding freeze-frame. Use the words 'Action' and 'Freeze' to start and stop the freeze-frames and improvisation work.

Preparation

Make one copy per child of photocopiable page 134. Make one copy of photocopiable page 135 per group for the extension activity aimed at the more confident children. Clear a space to make an acting area if using the classroom for this activity.

Resources needed

Photocopiable pages 134 and 135, an acting area.

What to do

Give each child a copy of photocopiable sheet 134. Talk about what the children think is happening in the picture and what might happen next. For example, the teacher in the picture may ask the children playing if they have fallen out with the sad child, or the children may go over to the child to ask what is wrong. Ask some children to make a freeze-frame of the picture using the acting area, and to show this to the class.

Discuss what each person might say if the freeze-frame were brought to life for a short while and talk about what might happen as a result of this conversation. Then ask each character in the demonstration group to decide on the first thing they will say when the freeze-frame comes to life. Explain that each character will say something in turn to start off the improvisation, then they can continue the improvisation, speaking in any order they wish. (This ensures that every child in the group has a chance to speak.) The characters should continue talking until you say 'Freeze', when they should make a final freeze-frame.

Make it clear that when the freeze-frame comes to life, the characters will be free to say whatever they like, as long as it makes sense and is not rude or silly. Stress also that no-one is to do anything dangerous like falling over or pushing. Now bring the demonstration group's freeze-frame to life, letting the improvisation run for a few minutes or until the characters run out of things to say.

After this, put the children into groups of three and ask them to make up their own improvisations based on the picture. Explain that each performance should be fairly short and that the same rules apply as in the demonstration. Some children may want to say less than others, and it may be worth pointing out that no-one should feel forced to say more than they wish to. Go round the groups and support those who need it. Groups who work quickly can be asked to add something else to their improvisation to make it more interesting.

Performance ideas

Display a variety of interesting photographs or paintings featuring groups of people. (Paintings by artists such as LS Lowry are particularly suited to this kind of work.) Let the children work in their groups to make freeze-frames of people in the pictures and to turn these into improvisations. The improvisations can be polished up and extended before performing as short plays with simple props and costumes.

Reference to photocopiable sheets

Photocopiable page 134 provides a picture of a simple playground scene as a stimulus for the children's improvisations. Photocopiable page 135 includes a picture of a birthday party scene and is intended to extend the improvisation activity for more confident children.

When the groups have finished, allow them to have a final run through. Then let each group perform their improvisation to the rest of the class. Ask the children watching to pick out the things they liked best about a performance before moving on to look at the next one.

Suggestion(s) for extension

Use photocopiable page 135 as an extension for the more able children. This provides a picture of a birthday party as a stimulus for further group improvisation. Encourage the children to include as much detail in their dialogue as possible and to be imaginative in their improvisation of the birthday party scene.

Suggestion(s) for support

Use mixed-ability groups to support less confident children. Encourage them to say short sentences that they will remember. Children who are not able to take part verbally can be given a non-speaking part involving specified actions.

Assessment opportunities

Note any children who are able to initiate ideas or develop those of others. Look out for children who make little contribution to group discussions and those who find it difficult to speak in front of an audience.

DRAMA

THE BOX

To use simple objects as props to stimulate spontaneous improvisation.

†† *Small groups working in front of the whole class.*

🕐 *30 to 45 minutes.*

Previous skills/knowledge needed
Some experience of spontaneous improvisation in large and small groups is needed (see 'Shopping centre' on page 49).

Key background information
Children should be asked to volunteer to take part in improvisations. Do not force reluctant or shy children. Those who are less confident can be invited to contribute through initiating ideas. Keep each improvisation short and simple.

It is important to remember that this activity is intended to build confidence in devising and performing rather than creating a play.

Preparation
Clear an area for acting if using the classroom. Fill a box with the objects listed below and place to one side of the space.

Resources needed
An acting area, six to ten objects to stimulate improvisations, such as: a telephone, a handbag containing a purse, a bunch of keys, a wallet, a birthday card, a camera, a remote control device, a gardening tool, some chalk, a shoe, and so on; a box to contain these objects.

What to do
Sit everyone together and invite a child to pick an object from the box. Ask the class to help you think of a sentence with the name of this object in it. For example: *'I must phone my friend'* or *'I can't find my keys'*. Ask the children who might say this sentence and why. Use the object to build a situation and ask for one or two volunteers to act this out in front of the class. Start on the word 'Action' and explain that the improvisation must stop when you say the word 'Freeze'. Make it clear that no-one is to say anything that is rude or silly, or do anything dangerous such as hitting or pushing. Involve more children as the situation develops, but be aware that too many participants can split the focus and lead to confusion. Between two and five performers at any one time usually works best.

Now repeat this activity using a different object and different children each time. Let the class make most of the decisions about each situation as they gain confidence.

Suggestion(s) for extension
Give one or two objects to the groups. Ask them to make up their own improvised situations using their object(s). These can be performed to the rest of the class.

Suggestion(s) for support
Join in the improvisations to support less confident children. If you have to take the major speaking role, try to involve these children by asking them to perform actions, such as making tea or writing down a phone message on an imaginary pad.

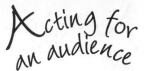

Assessment opportunities

Look for those children who can use the objects with imagination while noting those who lack confidence in their performance but can initiate imaginative ideas for others. Note also any children who are able to choose appropriate words with precision and show an awareness of the needs of the audience. Look out for children who are able to think on their feet and react spontaneously in a role-play situation.

Performance ideas

Select one of the improvisations and work with the class to develop it into a more substantial narrative. Let the whole class or a small group develop this into a short play suitable for performing to a wider audience.

Display ideas

Set out a variety of objects on a table for pairs of children to use as a stimulus for further improvisations.

REHEARSING THE SCHOOL PLAY

To build confidence in performing to a large audience.

†† *Whole class and pairs.*

⏲ *20 to 60 minutes, depending on the play and the allocated rehearsal time.*

Previous skills/knowledge needed

Children need to be familiar with the storyline or sequence of events in the chosen play.

Key background information

Taking part in a school play can be a valuable learning experience for children, but rehearsals can often cause stress and anxiety for everyone involved. These activities are designed to ease the process, through an emphasis on structure, focus and enjoyment. Good organization and communication are vital to the smooth running of rehearsals and you should start in plenty of time.

Prior knowledge of the whole play is important for all the children, even if your class is only involved in part of the play. If you intend to use a commercially produced play, choose one which can be adapted to suit your own needs and one which will involve all the children. However, keep in mind that some of the best plays for children have been written by teachers.

Keep spoken lines short and adapt them to suit the children if necessary. Some of the best dialogue comes from improvised situations where the children have been allowed to make up their own words to the play's storyline. Improvised dialogue can be adapted and integrated into an existing play or it can be scripted to form the whole play. Children are more likely to remember a script if it has been created in this way and they may be able to improvise if they forget their lines.

Preparation

Divide the chosen play (or the part of the play relevant to your class) into rehearsal units, involving one main incident or event. Copy and use the grid on photocopiable page 136 to record which characters you will need and other details for each unit. Plan your ideal timetable of rehearsals, but be prepared to be flexible. Organize your rehearsal space and, ideally, ensure some access to the performance area during the week leading up to the dress rehearsal.

Allocate parts to children based on your experience and knowledge of them rather than holding auditions. Find a part for everyone, whether it be a speaking or non-speaking part, or helping backstage. If you are using a play with a limited number of parts, create more by adding groups, such as passers by, friends, neighbours or crowds. Prepare a short summary of the main events in the whole play in language that the children will understand.

Resources needed
Photocopiable page 136, the chosen play script, a prepared outline of the story of the play, a rehearsal space, access to the performance area (see above).

What to do
Remind the children of the story of your chosen play by using the outline summary. Now concentrate on the part(s) of the play the children are going to perform and let them walk through what they do in the play, so that they get a sense of the order of events. Let this happen as you narrate the story, without the children speaking and without any detailed direction from you on acting skills. This is intended

to be lighthearted, enjoyable and fairly rapid, like a silent movie. It will inevitably be a little chaotic initially and will need to be repeated once more to be of benefit.

Rehearsals will be much more effective if you concentrate on one thing at a time. If the children have to learn lines, start this well in advance of the first rehearsal. Let them work in pairs to achieve this, so that they can test each other. Once the lines are learned, or moves for non-speaking parts understood, focus on the feelings in the play. This can be achieved by asking children questions as if they were in role, and by isolating key moments to talk about what the characters involved might have been feeling at the time. Involve the whole group in deciding how the characters will express these feelings on stage.

Focus on the technical aspects of acting last of all. These involve making sure the audience can see the characters at all times, working out exits and entrances, costume changes and voice projection. To help with this last item, organize the children into pairs and ask them to stand on opposite sides of the room to their partners. Let each child take a turn in saying a short line to their partner, imagining that they are talking across the stage. After each line is spoken, the children on the opposite side of the room must repeat the line in chorus, or the child's partner can repeat it. If it is repeated incorrectly, the child must say the line again, so that their partner can hear.

Next, put each pair closer together and ask them to say

Suggestion(s) for support

Give less able children short lines to speak, perhaps in chorus with another child. Try to find significant parts for less confident children, even if they do not involve speech. These could include bringing an important written message or object, acting as one of a pair of leaders in a procession or playing an assistant or friend who accompanies a main character.

Assessment opportunities

Focus on the children's acting skills and their ability to understand the needs of an audience. Note any children with confident, clear voices and good projection, as well as those for whom speaking in front of an audience is an ordeal. There is also the opportunity to assess the children's attitude to working as part of a team. Look out for children who attempt to help others with their performance or give support backstage, and note those who are sensitive to the feelings of others when making comments.

Opportunities for IT

If the school has a digital camera then pictures can be taken during rehearsals and these can be downloaded to the computer. The pictures can then be used within word processed work, in a number of ways:

▲ A class diary of rehearsals with a written commentary written about what happened at each one
▲ A diary for a particular child, group or scene
▲ Captions for pictures which can be displayed in the class or around the school
▲ Part of a program or poster advertising the play
▲ As a basis for a newspaper style review or article about the play and its rehearsals.

Similar pictures could be created using a traditional camera and scanning the photographs. If the school has a Polaroid more instant results are available than if using a normal developing process.

a line to each other as though they are on stage. The rest of the group should stand as far away as possible and then repeat the lines to confirm they have been heard. During rehearsals, ask the children to identify who they are supposed to be talking to at any one time and encourage them to look in that person's direction as they speak. Ask them to imagine that they are talking to the top of that person's head, or over the heads of the audience if they are talking to the front.

Praise good practice and progress throughout the rehearsals to create an ethos of hard work and enjoyment. If there are children at rehearsals who are not directly involved, make sure they have plenty to do and stress the need for good manners when other children are acting.

Suggestion(s) for extension

Ask some groups to improvise their section of the play before learning the lines. This gives children a greater confidence and understanding of the events and feelings in the play. Invite them to adapt any lines to suit their needs, as long as they have valid reasons and the changes are incorporated into the script before others learn the cues.

Performance ideas

Perform the dress rehearsal to another audience, such as another class, the governors or the lunchtime supervisors.

Display ideas

Ask the class to draw pictures of the main events in the play and use these to create a storyboard. Put the storyboard

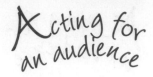

on display whenever rehearsals are taking place to act as a useful reminder. Take photographs of children in rehearsals and display these as ongoing work.

Reference to photocopiable sheet

Photocopiable page 136 provides a grid which the teacher can use for organizing and recording details of rehearsals. The grid can be duplicated as necessary to accommodate more rehearsal units.

Rehearsal grid			
Date and time	Place	Rehearsal unit number and brief description	Names of characters or groups of characters

PUPPETS ON THE MOVE

To give practice in manipulating puppets for performance.

†† *Small groups performing to the whole class.*

🕑 *5 to 10 minutes per group.*

Previous skills/knowledge needed

Children should have had the opportunity to play freely with the puppets without an audience.

Key background information

Poor manipulation of puppets can spoil attempts to put on a good puppet show for an audience. It is difficult to learn how to manipulate a puppet while also having to concentrate on following the story. These skills need to be separated so that children can begin to master handling the puppets effectively before moving on to perform a story.

Preparation

Put a curtain or sheet over a washing line, at a height just

above the children's heads. Arrange the classroom so that the children can sit as an audience facing the sheet. Make sure there is enough room for three or four puppeteers to stand behind the sheet and to each side. Make one copy of photocopiable page 137.

Resources needed

Photocopiable page 137, three or four simple hand-held or glove puppets, a washing line and a sheet or curtain, an acting area.

What to do

Sit the class in front of the sheet to form an audience. Organize the children into small groups of three or four ready for the activities described below. If necessary, select just a few of these activities in any one session, so that every child can have a turn. It is best to let each group attempt all the activities planned for the session before going on to let another group perform. Allow groups a maximum of three attempts at each activity before moving on to do the next one. The activities can be repeated at

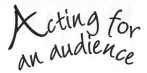
another time, if necessary. Stop any boisterous manipulation of the puppets by emphasizing the need to avoid damaging them.

The first activity involves moving the puppets along the sheet, without the puppeteers' hands or heads being seen. Involve the audience by inviting their opinions on how successful the puppeteers are in achieving this. The next activity involves the puppeteers taking turns to move their puppets along the sheet and back again, so that the audience can see the puppets' faces all the time. Then ask the puppeteers to walk their puppets backwards in a line along the sheet to the other side.

Follow this by asking the puppeteers to take turns in walking the puppets very slowly to one side of the sheet and then back again quickly, as if they are in a hurry. Next, ask them to make the puppets jump up and down in one place, without showing the children's own heads or hands. Now focus on walking the puppets as if they are feeling happy, then sad, then angry.

Let the whole class make suggestions on how to achieve this by considering how real people walk when feeling these emotions. Finish by asking the puppets to take a bow to audience applause.

Suggestion(s) for extension

Ask pairs of the more confident children to walk their puppets together and make them talk to each other as they go. Suggest that the puppets discuss something specific, such as what they will wear to a forthcoming party or what present they will buy a friend for his/her birthday.

Suggestion(s) for support

Vary the activities so that they can be differentiated to support groups or pairs of less confident children. Create a simplified version of the activities by explaining that not all puppets move behind a sheet or curtain. Invite the children to carry the puppets around the acting area in various different ways, as if they were walking alongside them.

Assessment opportunities

Assess children's progress in manipulating the puppets confidently and note those who work more imaginatively with their puppets to create some kind of character. Audience response is often a good indicator of success in this respect.

Performance ideas

Use photocopiable page 137 to incorporate some of the activities above into a short performance for some or all the groups to attempt with simple glove puppets which they could make themselves. Narrate the story, giving the children the opportunity to interpret the text by moving the puppets accordingly.

Display ideas

Let the children decorate their glove puppets and put them on display.

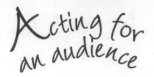

Reference to photocopiable sheet

Photocopiable page 137 provides a simple narrative to enable the children to use some of their newly acquired skills in the context of performing a story.

Puppet play: Sun, rain and wind

One sunny day *(name the puppets)* decided to go for a walk. It was very hot and so they walked very slowly.

(Pause until the first puppet reaches the end of the sheet.)

Suddenly, it started to rain, so they ran back home as quickly as they could.

(Let all the puppets go off the stage.)

The next day, it was cold and windy, but *(name the puppets)* decided to go for a walk anyway. Then it started to rain. They were feeling very sad without the sun. Suddenly, a strange thing happened. The wind died down, the rain stopped and the sun came out.

(Name the puppets) were feeling very happy as they walked back home in the sunshine. As they looked up at the sky, they saw a lovely rainbow. But they were not looking where they were going and suddenly, they all fell over and started to cry. They decided to sing a little song to cheer themselves up.

(Choose a song about the weather such as 'I Hear Thunder' by Max De Böo, Scholastic.)

Soon they felt a lot better and set off home feeling happy again. In fact they were so happy that every now and again, they gave a little jump to show just how good they felt about seeing the sun again. And that is the end of the story.

(Let all puppets go off stage and then reappear to take a bow as the class applaud them.)

Preparation

Set out the art materials on tables (see below). Cut out enough cardboard circles measuring about 30cms in diameter for one half of the class. Collect enough shoe boxes, without lids, for the other half. Cut one long side from each shoe box to make the shape of an enclosed stage. Make one copy per child of photocopiable sheet 138. Put some percussion instruments in a container.

Resources needed

Photocopiable page 138, a range of art materials, including scissors, glue, crayons, paints and pieces of fabric, cardboard, shoe boxes (without lids), cardboard circles (30cm in diameter), a story suitable for adding sound effects to, such as *One Stormy Night* by Ruth Brown (Red Fox), various simple percussion instruments and a box to contain them, theatre pictures and artefacts (for example, programmes, tickets, posters, leaflets, etc).

What to do
Introduction

Show the children your collection of theatre pictures and artefacts. Use these to open up a discussion on what to expect during the forthcoming theatre visit. Explain words such as 'stage', 'set', 'costume', 'stage curtains' and 'stage

WATCHING THEATRE

To extend children's understanding of theatre in preparation for a theatre visit.

†† *Whole class.*

🕐 *Approximately 60 minutes.*

Previous skills/knowledge needed

The children should be told about their forthcoming visit to the theatre. They should be familiar with the terms 'actors' and 'audience' through taking part in their own performances.

Key background knowledge

A theatre visit may be a totally new experience for many children but opportunities for learning can be missed through lack of preparation. These practical activities will help the children become more aware of what to look for on their visit, thus increasing their knowledge and enjoyment of the play. The activities introduce a basic theatre vocabulary which can be used to discuss the performance afterwards. This vocabulary can also be used during the visit to draw children's attention to aspects of the theatre and play.

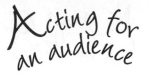
lights'. Remind the children of the terms 'actor', 'actress' and 'audience'. Talk about the use of music and sound effects. Read a simple story then show the children the box of percussion instruments. Ask them to pick out which ones might be suitable for providing sound effects if the story was performed as a play. Let some children try out the sounds. Finally, talk about costumes and scenery and discuss what would be appropriate for a play based on a well-known story, such as *Hansel and Gretel*.

Development

Now let half the class work at the cardboard circle activity, and half work at the shoe box activity (see below). Photocopiable page 138 should be completed by all the children after the practical activities.

The card circle activity: Discuss how some plays are performed on a round stage in the middle of the audience. Give each child a card circle to represent a round stage and ask them to prepare it for a play set in a garden. They can make the stage resemble a garden by colouring the card green and using scrunched tissue paper for bushes and plants. Blue paper can be used for a pond, but point out that the garden should not be too crowded as there needs to be plenty of room for the actors.

The shoe box activity: Give each child a shoe box and ask them to imagine that it is a stage for a play set in a garden outside a palace. Ask them to draw the palace onto the back of the stage and then use any other art materials to make the rest of the stage resemble the palace garden.

Conclusion

After the children have completed their practical activities and the photocopiable sheet, compare a round stage with a box stage and point out some of the advantages and disadvantages of each one. Explain that on the theatre visit, the children should look at the type of stage used. Ask them to notice how the stage is painted and decorated, what costumes the actors and actresses wear and any music and/or sound effects. The class can then discuss these things after the visit, along with the performance of the play itself.

Suggestion(s) for extension

Ask the more confident children to plan and then make an appropriate stage set for a particular story or part of a story. The shoe box stage would probably be best for this. Alternatively, two or three children could make sets for different parts of a familiar story. For example, a play of the

Snow White story would require a forest, the dwarves' cottage and the palace. Extend this by asking the children to design and draw costumes for the characters in the play.

Suggestion(s) for support

Simplify the practical activity by asking children to make the shoe box into a forest, using crayons, glue and pieces of fabric. This can be achieved by drawing trees on the

insides of the shoe box and colouring the base green and brown. Pieces of fabric can then be glued on for a more three-dimensional effect.

Assessment opportunities

Note which children make references to previous visits to the theatre and which children show limited knowledge of what to expect. Look out for children who can use the art materials confidently and produce imaginative stage sets.

Opportunities for IT

Some children might be able to use an art package to create the background scenes for their shoe box stage sets. These could be printed out and stuck onto the back of the shoebox. Children might also create stand up items, such as trees, in the same way. They could use the duplicate or cut and paste commands to make several trees very easily. Each one could then be personalized using slightly different colours, or by stretching and squashing to make them different sizes.

Performance ideas

Ask the children to perform freeze-frames of significant moments from the play they have seen (see 'Special moments' on page 14). Use these to stimulate further discussion about the play.

Display ideas

Display the children's stage sets together with the theatre artefacts and some of the completed photocopiable sheets. Use the display as a reference point for discussions after the theatre visit and add any subsequent work by the children concerning the play.

Reference to photocopiable sheet

Photocopiable page 138 gives children the opportunity to invent suitable costumes for different types of characters.

Personal and social development

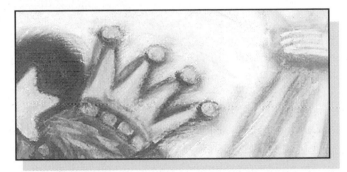

Drama is essentially a group activity which relies on co-operation and mutual understanding to succeed. Many drama exercises and games seek to develop such skills. Their aim is to improve the social health of the group in order to improve the quality of the drama work. This chapter includes some of these games and exercises, pitched at a level suited to the younger child. Taking part in a whole-group drama demands a deeper level of commitment, which can also contribute to children's personal and social development. Some of the imaginary situations in this chapter require the children to work together in a large group or in pairs to carry out the drama tasks.

Other activities in this chapter focus on exploring problems relating to specific personal and social issues, such as bullying, making friends and sibling rivalry. Drama offers a non-threatening way of tackling sensitive issues, allowing children to explore ideas from the safety of an imaginary context. In these activities, children are asked to support and advise various characters with problems, using their own experience to search for meanings and solutions.

There are several activities in this chapter which focus on helping people in trouble. These activities give important messages to children about the need to help other people for no reward, other than personal satisfaction in a job well done. Drama has much to offer in the area of personal and social development, but needs to be used consistently over a sustained period of time for maximum benefit. Any improvement drama can bring to the social health of the class and/or the children's self esteem will have a positive effect on the way children learn in all other areas of the curriculum.

DRAMA

PUPPETS WITH PROBLEMS

To use an imaginary context to stimulate improvisation on personal and social issues.

†† *Whole class.*

🕐 *20 to 30 minutes.*

Previous skills/knowledge needed
It would be helpful if the children had some previous experience of improvising stories in front of the class.

Key background information
The pictures on the photocopiable sheets suggest the four basic emotions of happiness, anger, fear and sadness. These help to develop children's awareness of different emotions in terms they can understand. This activity gives children the opportunity to explore these emotions in everyday contexts, within the safety of an imaginary situation. It uses a puppet with a problem to stimulate discussion by placing children in the role of experts giving advice. Conflicting or bad advice should be fully discussed in terms of the consequences and/or explored through the improvisations. The situations provide an excellent opportunity to develop children's skills in spontaneous improvisation.

Preparation
Clear an acting area if using the classroom and place the puppet or toy to one side. Make one copy of each of photocopiable pages 139 and 140. Paste these onto separate pieces of card and display them in or near the acting area.

Resources needed
Photocopiable pages 139 and 140, an acting area, an attractive puppet, doll or furry animal with a neutral face, two sheets of A4 card, glue.

What to do
Refer to the photocopied pictures on display and ask the children what each character is feeling. Use the pictures to focus on the four basic emotions of happiness, anger, fear and sadness and to discuss when people might feel them. Bring out the puppet and make it look upset. Make it communicate with the children through whispering to you. Tell the children about the puppet's problem. Use a situation within the children's own range of experience, such as happiness at receiving a new toy followed by sadness when it is lost or broken, fear of starting a new class or sleeping in the dark, anger at the behaviour of a baby brother or sister and so on. Then invite the children to give practical advice.

Translate one or two of the children's ideas into real situations improvised for the benefit of the puppet. Ask for volunteers each time and keep the situations short. For example, one child might role play an annoying baby brother, using experiences suggested by the class. Another child might role play the baby's elder sister as she makes a

DRAMA

number of suggested responses, such as trying to distract the baby or moving away. Try to conclude with some practical solutions for the puppet. Reward the children by making the puppet seem a little happier. Use the pictures again to identify and reflect on some of the feelings explored during the lesson.

Suggestion(s) for extension

Make the improvisation less prescriptive and more open-ended for the more confident children. Set the beginning of the improvisation and make a number of suggestions for how things might develop before allowing the children to take over. Keep control by telling them that they must stop when you say the word 'Freeze'.

Suggestion(s) for support

Differentiate through questioning during the activity. Ask less confident children suitable questions about the photocopied pictures and use 'either/or' type questions when asking them to give the puppet advice. Give support during improvisations by making the sequence of events clear and simple and by taking a role yourself to encourage verbal response.

Assessment opportunities

Look for children who make appropriate responses in role and are able to recall what has been decided about the content of the improvisations. Note children's ability to listen to the opinions of others and make relevant contributions to what is being discussed.

Opportunities for IT

The children could use an art package to create their own puppet faces to depict different emotions. These could be cut out and made into a class display. Some curriculum software like *Smart Alex* from Brilliant Computing enables children to create faces from a range of different parts and explore and develop vocabulary around them.

If the school has access to a digital camera the teacher or children could take pictures of the puppets during the activity. The pictures could be saved onto the computer and used in word processed work based on the activity.

Schools with access to e-mail could explore the use of combinations of different punctuation marks to give some form of emotion, for example:

:-)	a smiley face, happy
:- (	unhappy face, sad
:- D	a laughing face
; -)	a wink, joking face

Performance ideas

Some of the children's improvisations may be developed into a performance for an assembly on the theme of 'feelings'.

Reference to photocopiable sheets

Photocopiable pages 139 and 140 provide a visual focus for a discussion on the four emotions of happiness, sadness, anger and fear.

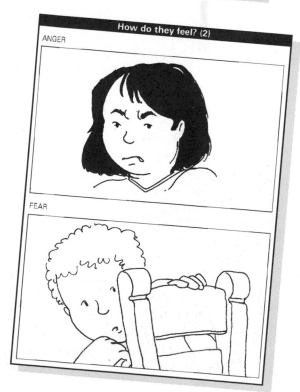

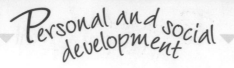

Display ideas

Let children make pictures of significant moments from the puppet's story and the improvisations. These can be displayed with accompanying sentences identifying some of the emotions involved, such as 'The puppet is feeling angry'. The photocopied pictures can be added to this display.

BULLIES IN FOCUS

To enable children to use freeze-frames as a focus for discussion.

†† *Whole class directing small groups.*

🕐 *30 minutes.*

Previous skills/knowledge needed

It would be helpful, though not essential, if the children had some previous experience of making class freeze-frames (see 'Special moments' on page 14). Some discussion beforehand on different kinds of bullying would also be an advantage.

Key background information

Acting out bullying situations can often lead to boisterous behaviour and a lack of sensitivity. Freeze-frames provide a means of exploring moments of tension and aggression without the need to act them out fully. Asking the children to identify the feelings of the characters involved encourages greater understanding about the issues. Using an imaginary situation also provides a safe framework within which to discuss the children's fears and challenge assumptions. It is important to keep the drama focused on the imaginary situation at all times.

Preparation

Clear a space to make an acting area. Make one copy of each of photocopiable pages 141 and 142. Paste each photocopy onto a separate sheet of A4 card.

Resources needed

Photocopiable pages 141 and 142, an acting area, two sheets of A4 card, glue.

What to do

Introduction: Setting the scene

Explain that you are going to tell the children the beginning of a story about a girl (or boy) called Jo, who didn't want to go to school. The story starts as follows:

When Jo was at school, some children made her feel very sad and no-one in her class would play with her. Jo didn't know what to do. She felt scared – too scared to tell anyone. When her mum and dad asked her why she didn't want to go to school, Jo told a lie and said she wasn't well. Then when the teacher asked her why she didn't want to go out to play, she lied again, still saying she was unwell. Jo was very sad.

Now show the class the first picture (photocopiable page 141). Tell the children that this shows what happened to Jo at school. Ask the class probing questions about what might

be happening in the picture. Can the children speculate on when, where and why this might be happening?

Development: Making freeze-frames

Now ask a few children to stand in the acting area. Let them make a version of the picture in a freeze-frame. Explain that they must do this by copying the way the people are standing in the picture. When you say the word 'Freeze', they must stand very still to create a 'frozen' picture. Ask the rest of the class to help decide how the children should be positioned to make the depiction as accurate as possible.

Before saying the word 'Freeze', ask the class how each person in the picture might have been feeling or thinking, at that particular moment. Encourage the children in the freeze-frame to take on the appropriate expressions. They should hold the freeze to the count of three, so that everyone sees clearly what is happening. Then repeat the whole activity using the other picture (photocopiable page 142), starting with a short discussion about what is happening in the picture.

Conclusion: Exploring solutions

Now ask the class to think about what Jo could and should do about her situation. Explore the children's suggestions by making freeze-frames to illustrate their solutions. Explore all of the children's suggestions in this way, concentrating on the feelings and consequences involved in each one. Eventually, try to reach a consensus of opinion on the best advice for Jo and incorporate this into the end of the story. For example:

The next day, Jo decided to tell the teacher. The teacher had a word with the bullies and told the whole class about how sad Jo had been. After this, some of the children in her class started to play with her. One of the bullies said she was sorry and promised never to bully her again.

If there is no consensus, use the children's main ideas, including the consequences of any poor advice. Try to end the story on a positive note.

Suggestion(s) for extension

Ask a group of more able children to prepare a freeze-frame of what happened the next morning at Jo's house when Jo didn't want to go to school. Invite the children to bring this new situation to life for a short while, including an improvisation of a dialogue between Jo and her parents. They should start and finish their improvisation with a suitable freeze-frame. The finished improvisation can be performed to the rest of the class if appropriate.

Suggestion(s) for support

Differentiate the questions to ensure that less confident children have an opportunity to express their opinions about the situations shown on the photocopiable pages. Use 'either/or' type questions if necessary and encourage these children to take part in the freeze-frames.

Assessment opportunities

Look for children who can identify feelings and show an awareness of the issues. Note those children who are able to think through solutions offered by others and explore the consequences. This lesson also provides an opportunity to assess children's confidence in working through the medium of a freeze-frame.

Opportunities for IT

The children could use a word processor to create and present a list of suggestions for dealing with bullies or getting help about being bullied. They would need to know how to change the size of the fonts and format them, possibly using the 'centre' command. Pictures could be added, scanned from the children's own line drawings, photographs or taken with a digital camera.

The digital pictures could be used as a focus for more extensive writing about a particular situation acted out in the classroom. The picture could be imported into the word processor or desktop publishing package and the children write about how the situation arose or how it was, or could be, resolved. They may need to know how to arrange text around the picture. In some word processors text can be set to 'flow' around the pictures, in others children will need to tab each line to a particular point or set up new margins. In simple desktop publishing packages a series of frames can be set up for the writing. For example:

Picture

The writing goes in here to start with

When the first box is full the writing goes into this frame

Display ideas
The photocopiable pictures can be displayed together with the children's own drawings of possible solutions to Jo's problem. The drawings can be based on the freeze-frames made during the lesson.

Reference to photocopiable sheets
Photocopiable pages 141 and 142 provide pictures of a situation involving bullying. The children use these to create their initial freeze-frames before suggesting various solutions which they also convey in freeze-frames.

What's happening? (1)

What's happening? (2)

ISLANDERS

To develop group co-operation skills through using a drama game.

†† *Whole class.*

🕐 *10 to 15 minutes.*

Previous skills/knowledge needed
None are required for this activity.

Key background information
The purpose of this game is for children to help each other, rather than compete with one other. The structure of the game also necessitates different groupings each time. This can be an excellent ice-breaker when working with new groups of children. It can also be used as part of a programme of activities to improve the social skills of a particular group.

Preparation
Place enough individual PE mats in a hall so that every child will have room to sit on part of a mat. Put some of the mats together to form islands and spread the others around the hall.

Resources needed
A hall or similar large space, PE mats.

What to do
Ask the children to sit on the mats. Encourage them to pretend that the mats are islands and that they are the islanders. Tell the following story as an introduction to the activity:

Every day, the islanders would go out to fish in the waters around the little islands. There were very few fish around these islands and it was difficult to track them down. The islanders had to row far out to sea to stand a chance of catching anything. The islanders had to keep rowing between the islands to catch enough fish. They used to share what they caught each day, so that everyone had enough to eat. The islanders needed everyone to help catch the fish or they would go hungry. They tried very hard to look after each other and they were allowed to go on any island they pleased.

Next, explain that on the word 'Action', the children must leave their 'islands' and pretend to move around the sea, catching fish. Say that you will narrate part of the story while they do this. Ask them to walk around the islands, pretending to be in boats catching fish. Discuss how this might be mimed and come to some agreement about what will be acceptable. Reinforce the message that they must fish out at sea, not near the islands. The children must keep fishing until they hear you say *'then everyone went home'* as part of the narration. When they hear you say this, they must slowly return to an island. Stress that they can return to any island, since the islands belong to everyone.

Now say 'Action' to start the activity and narrate while the children are fishing. Use the following narration or make up your own:

It was a beautiful day as everyone went out to fish. The islanders rowed right round all the islands before they decided where to fish. Some caught fish straight away and some had to wait. Some caught big fish and put them in a net. Some caught little fish and put them in a bucket. Some caught shellfish and put them in a box. Soon, they had caught enough fish and then everyone went home.

At this point the children should return to their islands by sitting down on the mats. They must then listen to what happened next in the story:

One day, when the islanders were out fishing, a storm blew up and flooded two of the smaller islands. The islands disappeared into the sea. The islanders were sorry to lose two of their islands but were very glad that no-one was hurt. They didn't want to lose any of their friends.

Mirror this event by taking away two small mats and asking the children sitting on these to move to another 'island'. Start the fishing activity again, but stress that when the children return to the islands, they may have to stand on the mats in order to fit everyone on. Ask them to make sure that everyone has room to do this. This encourages them to co-operate with each other to make space for everyone.

Repeat the storm sequence several times, taking away more mats each time. Carry on until the children have to stand very closely together on the mats in order to accommodate everyone. This encourages group cohesion and co-operation by necessitating physical closeness and contact.

Conclusion

Finish with a brief discussion about the importance of co-operation and helping other people. Ask the children why we need to do this for one another. For example, what would have happened to the islanders in the story if their friends had refused to help them? How would the islanders involved have felt if anything bad had happened to their friends? Finish by discussing any occasions when the children have co-operated with someone by offering their help – for example, sharing in preparations for a holiday or for a visit from a friend or relative.

Suggestion(s) for extension

This activity can be made more challenging by adding a further problem of hurricanes approaching at sea. Explain to the children that these happen while the islanders are out fishing. Blow a whistle to warn them that the winds are coming. When they hear this, they have three seconds to return to the nearest island for safety. Those children who do not have their toes on a mat by the count of three are said to be drowned at sea and should sit out. Every islander lost in a hurricane counts as a point against the class. The game can be repeated to see if the class can improve on their last score.

Suggestion(s) for support
Let the less confident children fish in pairs to look after each other. Pair up reticent children with those who are more confident and let those who find co-operation difficult work with those who can share well. Ensure that there is always a realistic chance to accommodate everyone on the mats.

Assessment opportunities
Look for children who go out of their way to help others find an island and those who make room for others on their mat. This is also a good opportunity to assess children's skill and imagination in terms of mime work.

Display ideas
Ask each child to draw and cut out a picture of themselves on a small piece of card. Put the pictures into small groups and cut out a paper island for each group, making each one large enough to accommodate every picture from each group. Let each child paste their figure onto their group's island and then together, invent a name for the islands as one community. The islands can be displayed in a group, separated by sea. The children can draw their boats moored around each island.

ALL CHANGE!

To support drama work by developing group awareness and identity.

†† *Whole class.*

🕐 *20 to 30 minutes.*

Previous skills/knowledge needed
None are required for this activity.

Key background information
Drama is essentially a social activity and classes with poor social skills are disadvantaged in terms of what they can achieve. The two games here focus on knowledge and observation within the group to help create a sense of group identity. The first game is not intended to be competitive and children should be encouraged to change places slowly, with due regard to others.

Preparation
Arrange enough chairs for one per child in a large circle.

Resources needed
Chairs and enough space to accommodate them (see above).

What to do
Changing chairs
Ask the children to sit on the chairs in the circle. Ask everyone to hold up their left hand and check that they have done this correctly. Explain that on the word 'Go', everyone must move to sit in the chair nearest to their left hand. Repeat this a few times until the children can change places without fuss. Now call two children by name and ask them to change places. Repeat this a few times with different children.

Next, ask the children to put up their hands if they like red. Explain that when you say 'Go', all the children who like red must stand up and move to another chair. Repeat this with several different colours. Don't worry if all the children move each time. Then extend this activity to more specific things, such as those who have dark hair, blue eyes, shoes with laces or a name beginning with a certain letter.

What's changed?
Ask a pair of children to stand where they cannot see or hear the rest of the class. The pair should remain in this

place until they are told to return to the group. Explain that when they return, one pair in the circle will have changed something about their clothes. Give them some examples, such as shoes on the wrong feet, a jumper on back to front, a shoe lace or a buckle undone, one sock missing or one pair of hair ribbons missing. Tell them that they will be given a few minutes to guess what has changed.

While the chosen pair are away from the group, choose two children who are not sitting together to change a few simple things about their appearance. Then ask the other pair to return and tell them which two children have changed something. Give them a time limit of a couple of minutes to guess what has changed. Repeat the activity with different children each time.

Suggestion(s) for extension

Write the statements/questions for the 'changing chairs' game on cards and invite good readers to read them out for you. Invite more able children to guess by themselves what has changed instead of working in a pair.

Suggestion(s) for support

Support less able children in the 'changing chairs' game by marking out their left and/or right hands with stickers if necessary. Move through the activities slowly and make sure that the children are clear about when to move and

what to do each time. Pair them up with those who are more confident when doing the guessing in the 'what's changed?' game.

Assessment opportunities

Look for children who find it difficult to co-operate within a large group activity. This will be evident in the 'changing chairs' game if children try to race to another chair without regard for others.

Opportunities for IT

The children could use simple graphing software to create a pictorial representation of their ideas about what has changed. The data could be collected by a child or the teacher on a photocopied tally chart and then entered into the computer when the activity has finished. If the game is played several times different groups of children could take responsibility for producing the 'what's changed' graph each time. The children could experiment with different types of graphs to present the findings.

Display ideas

Represent the answers to the questions in the 'changing chairs' activity in the form of pictographs or block graphs. These can make an interesting display to complement the focus on group awareness.

DRAMA

COPYING

To support drama work by developing group co-operation skills and awareness.

†† *Whole class.*

🕐 *30 to 45 minutes.*

Key background information

The 'spot the leader' game in this activity relies on the co-operation of the whole group to make it work. It provides a sound basis for future drama work by helping to build a sense of group identity. It can be used to help children with low self-esteem or low status in the group by giving them opportunities to lead.

Preparation

If necessary, prepare the allocated space to make it suitable for movement activities.

Resources needed

A copying activity or game such as 'Punchinello', in *Action Rhymes and Games* by Max De Bóo (Scholastic), a large space.

What to do

Introductory games

Sit with the children in a circle. Conduct a straightforward copying activity such as repeating simple hand claps or movements, or playing games such as 'Punchinello' (see 'Resources'), where one child stands in the centre of the circle and invents an action for the others to copy.

Follow by developing this into a game called 'Fast, slow, stop', where one child standing in the middle of the circle invents actions which are either fast or slow. The child says 'Fast' or 'Slow' just before they start the action, then the other children try to copy the action. The class continues to be led by the child who calls out the instructions 'Fast', 'Slow' or 'Stop'. For example, a child might call 'Fast' and then swing one arm very fast, then suddenly call 'Slow' and swing their arm very slowly. He/she may then call 'Fast' and jump up and down quickly before calling 'Stop'. Emphasize that the class will need to concentrate carefully to keep up with copying the actions. The children should take turns to be the child in the middle.

Development: Follow the walk

Ask the children to follow you around the room in a line, copying whatever movements you make as you go. Make this a short activity but vary the movements to include walking, skipping and marching. Now put the children into

pairs and let them take turns to lead their partner around the room in a similar way. Tell them to move carefully to avoid others. Use a clear signal for stopping and starting, such as 'Action' and 'Freeze'.

Spot the leader

Now sit in a circle again and ask the children to copy whatever you do until you say 'Stop'. Warn them that they must concentrate, as you will keep changing what you do. Remain in the circle, but use a variety of small movements such as crossing and uncrossing your legs, scratching your head, looking in different directions, rubbing hands, clicking fingers, etc. Then ask for a volunteer to be the leader in a similar way.

Once the children can do the above activity reasonably well, introduce the following game. One child should stand away from the group so they cannot see what is happening. You should then silently point to a child in the circle to appoint them as leader. Whatever the leader does, everyone must copy. Make it clear that the leader must keep changing the movement every few seconds. As the leader starts off the first movement, the child standing out is asked to return and to try to guess who the leader is. Stop the activity after about half a minute and give the child two guesses. Discourage children from guessing too soon by telling them

DRAMA

partner first or help them yourself. Be prepared to reduce the time they spend leading if necessary.

Assessment opportunities
Observe the children's concentration levels when following a leader and look for leaders who show some awareness of the group when they move. Note also any leaders who show imagination in their selection of movements. It is also possible to assess the observational skills of those children who try to guess the leader.

Performance ideas
Sequences of identical movements by the class can be turned into an amusing performance which is also good for group cohesion.

GRANDAD'S GARDEN

To encourage children to work as a group to act out a simple story.

†† *Whole class.*

🕐 *30 to 45 minutes.*

Previous skills/knowledge needed
Some basic movement experience is needed, such as finding and working alone in a space and moving as different creatures or plants. A basic understanding of how plants grow from seeds would also be helpful.

Key background information
This short movement exercise provides children with an opportunity to work as a team to act out a sequence of imaginary events. The story on the photocopiable sheet requires children to make physical contact with each other in a sensitive and controlled manner. This helps create a sense of group satisfaction and trust, both of which are necessary if groups are to achieve their full potential in drama work.

Preparation
Make one copy of photocopiable page 143.

Resources needed
Photocopiable page 143, a large space, two tambourines, a scarf suitable for an elderly man, a young child's coat, a chair.

What to do
Begin by discussing how seeds are planted, then explain that you would like the children to mime this process to the words you are about to narrate. Use the following narration or make up your own, leaving adequate pauses for the children's mimes:

to wait until the activity has finished. Repeat the game with different children guessing and different children taking the lead each time. If a leader fails to keep changing their movements, give the child who is guessing another turn with a different leader.

Suggestion(s) for extension
Ask confident leaders to include more subtle movements, such as twitching the nose, winking, licking the lips or moving the fingers. Choose an equally confident child as the one who has to guess the leader.

Suggestion(s) for support
Let some children work in pairs to guess the leader. Give less confident leaders time to decide at least two movements beforehand. Let them plan this quietly with a

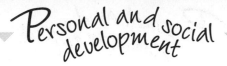

The children wanted to make some plants grow. They started by digging several small holes in the earth... then they carefully placed the seeds in the holes. They covered the seeds with soil... and patted them down with their hands. Finally, they found a watering can and gave the seeds some water.

The next part of the story will be as follows:

The little seeds lay under the ground for what seemed like a very long time... Then, as the weather started to become warmer, the seeds slowly began to grow... They grew bigger and bigger and bigger, until they became huge plants that covered the ground.

Before reading this part of the story, ask the children to find a space and curl up very small like the tiny seeds in the ground. Explain that when you play a tambourine, they should start to grow bigger. Encourage them to grow very slowly and then spread out their arms and legs like a growing plant. They should keep growing until they are as big as possible. Introduce a word or sound as a signal to stop. Now repeat the activity, but this time ask the children to move in response to your narration of the above story.

Now talk about how rain and sunlight help seeds to grow into plants. Ask the children to decide on suitable movements to depict the rain and the sun. Then let them make these movements into a short narration, such as:

The rain fell lightly at first... then it grew heavier and heavier... until suddenly, it stopped... and the sun came out.

Talk about insects that like to be near plants. Ask each child to think of an insect and how it moves. Explain that when you play the tambourine, they must move around the room like this insect approaching or climbing up a large plant. Give them a short time to try this, then stop playing. Discuss the birds that fly and land near plants and ask the children to think about how they might imitate these. Play the tambourine again, encouraging them to move like birds. Stop again and talk about cats that like to sit in the shade of large plants. Ask one or two children to demonstrate moving like sleepy cats towards the shade of a plant. Then let everyone try this as you slowly play the tambourine.

Now sit the children in a large circle. Join the circle and place the chair, scarf and coat beside you. Read aloud the story (i.e. the words in italics) on photocopiable page 143 and discuss how the children will act this out. (The suggestions on the sheet provide a guide for this.) Choose two children to represent Grandad and Gemma. The male and female roles can be changed round if necessary, to make the story about a boy called Jim and his grandmother. Then choose four children to be insects, four to be birds and two to be cats. Ask one child to be the seed and explain that the rest will be the stems and leaves of the plant when the seed grows. Let Grandad and Gemma play the tambourines to direct the movement. Go through the movements and directions slowly before trying to perform the story as a whole.

Suggestion(s) for extension
When discussing possible movements for the story, improve the group's work by asking the more confident children to demonstrate ideas for them to copy.

Suggestion(s) for support

Suggest that children look at others if they are unsure about how to move and encourage them to help each other. Create a sense of shared enterprise rather than individual excellence. Allow pair work to support the less confident children.

Assessment opportunities

Look for children who show imagination when interpreting the story through movement. Also note any children who make suggestions to improve the work of the group as a whole and those who attempt to support others.

Performance ideas

With a little rehearsal and the addition of some simple costumes and a few more percussion instruments, this activity can make a pleasing performance for the whole class to perform to a wider audience.

Display ideas

Ask the children to draw pictures and write information about the growing seeds and plants to form part of a project on plants and growth.

Reference to photocopiable sheet

Photocopiable page 143 provides a simple story script (and clear instructions) which forms the context for the movement activity.

The story of Grandad's garden

Gemma's grandad was feeling very sad.
(Grandad puts on the scarf and sits in his chair looking sad.)
His new bungalow had no garden. There was a small patch of bare earth in front of his window, but that was all. One day, Gemma brought some seeds and some gardening tools to Grandad's bungalow.
(Gemma puts on her coat and mimes carrying the tools to the centre of the circle.)
She went to the small patch of earth outside Grandad's bungalow and planted the seeds.
(Gemma mimes planting the seeds and then returns to circle. The child chosen as the seed moves to where Gemma has been planting and curls up tightly.)
As the days passed, the rain fell on the bare earth outside Grandad's window.
(Gemma and Grandad play tambourines as the class make rain movements.)
The sun shone on the bare earth outside Grandad's window.
(Children make sun movements, reaching over towards the seed. Gemma and Grandad play the tambourines.)
One day, one of the seeds began to grow *(child who is the seed starts to move upwards).* As the days passed, it grew bigger.
(Let two children extend the plant by joining themselves to the child's arms. They should do this by gently making contact with part of the child's arm using their fingers.)
And it grew bigger.
(Repeat this phrase pointing to various children each time, as a signal that they must join on to an extended arm to make the plant spread outwards. Ask them to join on arms at both ends of the plant, so that it grows in both directions. They should make the plant grow in a curve rather than in a line.)
The plant was so big that it covered the bare earth outside Grandad's window. Then insects flew among the leaves of the plant. *(Insects fly around.)* Then birds flew around the plant *(birds fly around),* and after that, some cats came to lie in the shade of the plant *(cats creep under the leaves).* When Grandad looked out of his window he was really pleased. He went to his cupboard, took out a small watering can and filled it with water from the tap.
(Grandad looks pleased and steps into the edge of the circle to mime the actions.)
He took the watering can to the piece of earth outside his window and watered the plant. *(Grandad walks around the plant to water it.)*
When Gemma came back to visit, Grandad smiled a great big smile, and so did Gemma.
(Gemma arrives and they both smile.)

ON THE FARM

To encourage children to work collaboratively in role.

†† *Whole class and pairs.*

🕐 *Session One: 15 to 20 minutes. Session Two: 30 to 40 minutes.*

Previous skills/knowledge needed

It would be helpful if the children had some understanding of small farms, and an appreciation of what is involved in looking after animals and crops.

Key background information

This activity works to develop social skills within a dramatic framework by encouraging group collaboration and helping those in need. The section involving teacher-in-role as a farmer can be substituted with a note from the farmer, asking for the children's help. While a note could be used to outline the problem and request help, teacher-in-role is the best strategy in terms of emotional impact. Session One can be carried out in a classroom, but Session Two needs a large space. As Session One is intended as an introduction to Session Two, the gap between them both should be as short as possible.

Preparation

For Session One, make one copy per child of photocopiable page 144. For Session Two, make a sign from A4 card saying 'Open' on one side and 'Closed' on the other. Make another sign saying 'Redhill Farm'. Prop up the 'Open' sign on a chair or ledge and put the farm sign on a nearby wall. Place the scarf near the signs. Write a thank you letter from the farmer, similar to the one following.

Redhill Farm
Hillstown

Dear Children

Thank you so much for helping me at the farm. I was feeling ill and you helped to make me feel better. I know that the animals would have been left without food and water and the jobs would not have been done if you had not helped. I liked the way you all worked together to do the jobs. We all have to work together on the farm and I am glad to say that my farm worker is now feeling better and is a great help.

When children come to the farm I tell them about how helpful you were. Please call in again sometime. Thank you once again. You are the best visitors we have ever had on our farm.

Best wishes

from the farmer

Resources needed

Photocopiable page 144, writing and drawing materials, two sheets of A4 card, a scarf suitable for a farmer, a large space (for Session Two).

What to do
Session One

Begin by talking about what jobs farmers need to do on small farms, then give each child a copy of photocopiable page 144. Read through the sheet to make sure everyone understands what to do and ask each child to complete it.

When they have finished, ask for volunteers to demonstrate how their farm jobs might be mimed.

Next, talk about how farm workers often work together on their jobs and discuss how some of the jobs might be carried out in pairs. Explain that this could involve working alongside each other on the same job, such as collecting eggs, or helping each other to complete a job, such as one person holding a fence post in the ground while the other hammers in the nails. Put the children into pairs and ask them to mime doing their jobs together. Look for pairs who are working collaboratively on a job and ask them to perform their mimes to the class.

Session Two

Sit the children at the side of the room opposite the farm signs. Ask if they will join you in pretending that the room is a farm and that they are going on a farm visit. Draw their attention to the signs and explain that these are hanging outside the farmhouse door. Say that the scarf near the door belongs to the farmer and ask them not to touch it. Define the parts of the room that are to be used in the story. Then ask the children to suggest what special outdoor clothes they should wear on their farm visit and let them mime putting these on.

Now start the story as a narration with the words:

'Once upon a time, a group of children from .... school, went to visit a farm, and this is what happened...'

Talk as if the visit were really happening and organize the children to walk up to the farm with their partners in a crocodile formation. Lead the way round the room, pointing out farm animals and other things as you walk. This journey should be brief, involving no more than two trips around the room. Stop outside the 'farmhouse door' and point out that the sign says the farm is open. Tell the children to sit down on the grass while you fetch the farmer.

Now ask the children to listen and watch as you act out what happens next in the story. Explain that you will pretend to be the farmer when you put on the scarf, but you will return to being yourself when you take it off. Then put on the scarf and change the sign to 'Closed'. Take on the role of a farmer who is feeling sad and unwell and cannot carry

out all the farm jobs. Explain that your farm helper is also ill and this is the reason you have had to close the farm to visitors. Ask the children for their help.

Ask the children if they know what jobs need to be done on a small farm like yours and listen to their ideas. Add other jobs if the list is short. Explain that the jobs must be carried out in pairs, and they should work with the partner they walked to the farm with. Warn them not to run around the farm and tell them to carry out the jobs carefully. Ask them if you can watch to make sure the jobs are done properly. Either let pairs of children carry out any job that needs doing, or allocate particular jobs to particular pairs.

Walk around to praise and encourage any examples of collaborative work as the children do their jobs. Stop any inappropriate behaviour by talking to the children about the need for behaving sensibly on your farm. If some children finish well before the others, give them other jobs such as fixing your gate or digging up vegetables.

When most children have made a good attempt at the jobs, call them to sit on the imaginary grass in front of your house. Take a brief walk around the farm to examine the work. Praise the general standard of work as you walk and then change the 'Closed' sign to say 'Open' once again. Thank the children and take off the scarf to come out of role. Make it clear that you are now back to being the teacher and comment on how kind the children have been and how well they worked together to carry out the jobs.

Organize the children into a crocodile formation again and set off on the walk back home. When you reach the end of the walk, sit everyone down and suggest that they take off their outdoor clothes. Ask them to pretend that after the visit, they received a letter from the farmer. Read out the thank you letter you have prepared. Explain that this is the end of the story about the farm visit. Finish by asking the children to pick out the part they liked the best and use this to reflect on the experience out of role.

Suggestion(s) for extension

Differentiate by demanding more detailed answers from confident children when discussing how best to mime and share the jobs. Ask some confident readers to read out the farmer's thank you letter to the class.

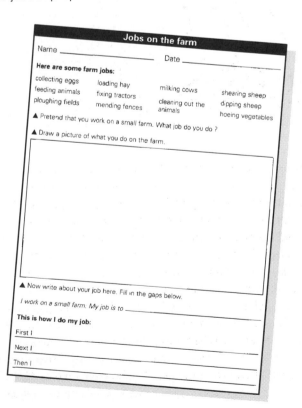

Suggestion(s) for support

Pair up a child needing support with a more confident child and let them complete one photocopiable sheet between them in Session One. Support the less confident children through your role as the farmer by talking to them and making suggestions as they carry out the jobs.

Assessment opportunities

Look for children who attempt to collaborate with each other and those who show concern for the farmer's problems. Notice how well children can recall details of the farm jobs when working for the farmer. This activity also provides an opportunity to assess children's ability to respond appropriately in role, using both mime and speech.

Performance ideas

Different jobs can be performed by groups of children in an agreed order, under the title: 'The day we helped a farmer'.

Display ideas

Make a display of the farm jobs using pictures drawn by the children and including the thank you letter from the farmer.

Reference to photocopiable sheet

Photocopiable page 144 provides an opportunity for the children to select a particular farm job and consider what kind of actions it would involve. This helps them to mime the jobs in preparation for Session Two.

THE LONELY PRINCE

To enable children to explore issues of friendship within a dramatic context.

†† *Whole class and small groups of three.*

🕐 *Session One: 15 to 20 minutes. Sessions Two to Five: 30 to 45 minutes.*

Previous skills/knowledge needed

The children should understand what a palace is and be capable of working in small groups for short spaces of time. They should also be familiar with the freeze-frame strategy (see 'Special moments', on page 14) and the words 'Action' and 'Freeze' as starting and stopping signals for drama.

Key background information

This activity is divided into five sessions, each of which should be separated by no longer than a week. Two of these sessions consist of practical drama activities, while the other three sessions focus on related writing and art work. Sessions Two and Four need a large space. Sessions One and Two aim to build belief in the imaginary situation to motivate children to solve the problems they will encounter in Session Four. Session Five forms a conclusion and provides an opportunity for the children to reflect on the issues involved. It is difficult for any learning to take place in drama without some opportunity for reflection and analysis. This can take place during the drama itself or soon afterwards and is an essential part of the process. The final task should therefore not be regarded as optional follow-up work.

Preparation

For Session One, make one copy of photocopiable page 145 for each group. For Session Three, make one copy of photocopiable page 146 per child.

Resources needed

Session One: Photocopiable pages 145, one pencil per group. Session Two and Four: A large space, a whistle, an adult-sized cloak. Session Three: Photocopiable page 146, writing materials. Session Five: Drawing materials for each child, an envelope large enough to contain all the children's drawings.

What to do

Session One

Tell the children that you are going to narrate a drama story about some servants who work in a palace kitchen belonging to a king and queen.

Ask the class if they will pretend to be the servants in the drama. Emphasize that they will need to act like grown-ups who have jobs working in the palace kitchen. Tell the children that the King and Queen have a son who everyone

calls the Prince. He is about the same age as the children and next week it will be his birthday. The Prince will be inviting all his friends to his birthday party and the King and Queen will also be there.

Explain that the story begins with the servants getting things ready for the Prince's birthday party. Tell the children that the servants work together in groups to do all the jobs for this. Organize the class into groups of three and give each group a copy of photocopiable page 145. Explain that the King and Queen have chosen the Prince's favourite foods for the party and the servants have made a list of everything they need to prepare for this. Read through the lists on the photocopiable sheet. Then ask the groups to fill in their sheet so they know which three jobs they will mime when they play the servants. Make it clear that members of a group should do the same jobs. After the sheets have been completed, ask groups to demonstrate their mimes. Let them do this two groups at a time if you have a large class.

Session Two

Ask the children to sit at the side of the hall in their groups of three. Ask them to pretend that the hall is the palace kitchen where the party will take place. Stress that it is a very large kitchen because there are many people living in the palace. Define the exact area to be used and point out anything that is out of bounds. Make it clear that the kitchen contains several cookers, many cupboards and all the cooking and cleaning things a large palace needs. However, it will be up to the children to decide exactly where things are.

Remind the children that the story will start with the servants making preparations for the Prince's birthday party next week. Remind them that they should mime the jobs and explain that they should talk to each other as if they really were the servants in the kitchen. Ask them to suggest what they might say to each other in the kitchen, then let the groups decide which job they will each do first. Tell everyone to fold their arms when they have decided.

Explain that the drama will start with a frozen moment, like a freeze-frame. The moment will occur as the servants are about to start their first jobs. Give the children a few seconds to discuss where and how their group will stand in the freeze-frame. Stress the need to choose a comfortable position that they can hold still for a few seconds and ask them to fold their arms when they have decided. When everyone is ready, send them out into the imaginary kitchen a few groups at a time to make the freeze-

frame. Keep any over-enthusiasm in check by explaining that the King and Queen forbid running in the kitchen because it is too dangerous.

Explain that when you say the word 'Action', the servants must come to life, and when you blow the whistle and say 'Freeze', they must stop as if frozen once more. Bring the drama to life on the word 'Action' and observe the class carefully. If any children need reminding about running, have a quiet word with them, rather than calling out during the drama as this will interrupt the flow of the work and spoil the building of belief. If there is a problem involving several children, then freeze the action and deal with it out of role. Let the activity carry on for as long as most children are absorbed in what they are doing. Eventually, freeze the action and gather the children together in their groups at the side of the room again.

Now ask half the class to return to their original freeze positions. Let them come to life again to perform some of the jobs they were doing for the other half of the class. Keep this short and after the performance ask the audience to guess what the jobs were. Then change over to let the other half of the class perform.

Gather the children into the middle of the imaginary kitchen area. Say that you are going to act out what happens next in the story. Explain that the servants are sitting in the kitchen having a break, when the royal messenger comes in, looking very worried. Say that you will play the part of the messenger when you put on the cloak. Ask the children

DRAMA

to pretend to be the servants again, but explain that they should just sit and listen rather than mime.

Now put on the cloak and announce to the servants that the Prince has lost all his party invitations. Explain that the King and Queen told the Prince to write some more but he doesn't want to and has gone away crying to his room. Say that the King now wants them, the servants, to write the invitations instead. As they won't know the names of the Prince's friends they will have to write 'Dear Friend' on each one, then fill in the date and time of the party and where it is to be held.

Explain that the children will return to the classroom to write their invitations. When the invitations are all completed, you the messenger will take them to the Prince so he can give them to his friends before the party. Then take off the cloak and come out of role.

Session Three

Return to the classroom and decide on a date and time for the party. Give each child some paper and a pen to write an invitation. When they are complete, collect the invitations together, then ask the class to speculate on reasons why the Prince didn't want to write his own invitations. Move on to discuss parties and how people invite special friends. Give each child a copy of photocopiable page 146 and read it through to ensure that everyone understands what to do. The children should fill in their own sheets but can discuss the work in their groups if they wish. When they have finished, discuss their responses and use this to open up a brief discussion on friendship.

Session Four

Give the invitations to a child and ask him or her to keep them in a safe place in the kitchen until the messenger arrives. Start the drama again with the children acting as servants making last-minute preparations for the party. Tell

them that at some point you will put on the cloak and enter the kitchen as the messenger. When that happens, the chosen child should fetch the invitations and everyone should sit down in front of the messenger to hear what the news is. Start with a freeze as before and bring it to life on the word 'Action'.

After a short time, enter as the messenger and take the invitations with a worried look. Thank the servants for writing them but explain that they will probably be of no use. Say that you have found out why the Prince lost his other invitations. Explain that he lost them on purpose because he doesn't want the King and Queen to know that

he has no friends. The Prince is very lonely. Lots of other royal children come to the palace to play but the Prince doesn't know how to make friends and sometimes he does things that other children don't like.

Say that, as the messenger, you are not sure exactly what the Prince is doing wrong, but he needs to know how to make friends before his party or no children will come. Ask the children what they think the Prince could be doing wrong and come to some agreement about the advice they should send him via yourself as the messenger.

After a short while, decide that it will be too difficult for the young Prince to remember all the things the servants have said. Ask them instead to make the Prince a little picture book showing how to make friends and how to make sure people will like you. Take off the cloak to come out of role. Talk about what pictures could be in the book and invite volunteers up to the front to make freeze-frames of possible pictures. Make one freeze-frame at a time, using different children for each one.

Session Five

Return to the classroom and let the children draw pictures for the book of advice on friendship. Ask them to include a sentence with their picture to explain their particular point about friendship. When finished, put the completed book in an envelope and ask the children to imagine that the messenger has taken it to the Prince. Explain that you will now tell the children what happens at the end of the story. Say that the Prince is very pleased with the book. The next day he goes to a cousin's seventh birthday party and tries out the advice. He makes lots of friends at the party and invites them all to his own party. He isn't sure if his new friends will come, but they do. Everyone used to call him 'the lonely Prince', but now they have given him the new name of 'the friendly Prince' – all because of the good advice he had from the servants' little book. Finish by saying that the Prince now keeps the book in a special place, to remind him of the kind servants who wrote it.

Suggestion(s) for extension

During Session Two, let small groups of more confident children show the others what they were discussing in the kitchen as they prepared for the party. This can be in addition to their performing with half the class. During Session Four, encourage these children to talk about friendship problems in more depth. Encourage confident writers to write longer passages of advice for the book in Session Five.

Suggestion(s) for support

If children need support during the birthday preparations in Session Two, take on a role as a servant yourself and work with these children as necessary. Let less confident children work in pairs with those who are more confident to write their invitation. In Session Five, the children can also work in pairs to support each other where necessary.

Assessment opportunities

Look for children who are able to work co-operatively with others in a role-play situation and those who will only work alongside others when put in a group. Note those children who listen to the opinions of others during discussions and make relevant comments in the light of what has been said. This activity also provides a good opportunity to assess how well the children understand how to write invitations.

Opportunities for IT

The children could use a word processor to write their own invitation cards for the Prince's party. They will need to decide what information is needed for the card and then how to arrange it to make the invitation look interesting. The children could add pictures taken from a clip art collection or drawn using an art package. They should be shown how to change the fonts and sizes to make the invitation look interesting. Discourage children from centering their text using the space bar but show them how to use the 'centre text' option on the word processor. Less competent writers could begin with the information already typed in and then decide how to format the text to personalize the invitation.

The children could also use a word processor or desktop publishing package to write their own class book of how to make friends. Each child or pair could be given a screen page on which to write their advice and add suitable pictures. The children will need to know how to add the picture, alter its size and move it around the screen. They will also need to be shown how to format the text to fit around the picture, or to start writing above or below it. The pictures could be drawn using an art package, taken

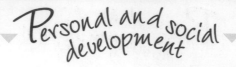
from a suitable clip art collection or scanned from the children's own line drawings. Children should also be shown how to save their work as they go so that it can be retrieved later for the class book.

Display ideas

Display the children's book of advice with other published books about friendship and behaviour, such as *What Feels Best* by Anita Harper and Susan Hellard (Picture Ladybird), *Bad Mood Bear* by John Richardson (Red Fox) and *Topsy and Tim and the Bully* by Jean and Gareth Adamson (Puffin).

Reference to photocopiable sheets

Photocopiable page 145 helps to prepare children for their roles as servants by suggesting what their jobs might involve at the start of the story. Photocopiable page 146 encourages them to think about issues of friendship in preparation for Session Four of the activity.

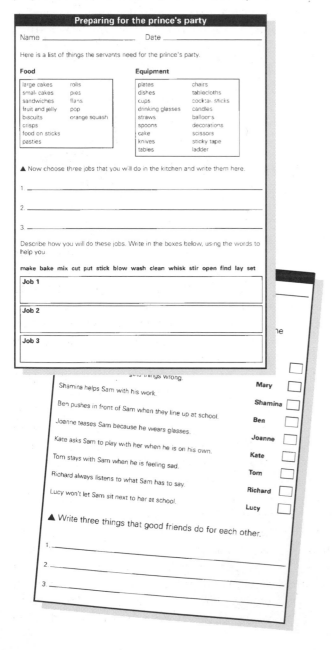

SANTA'S HELPERS

To provide an opportunity to take part in a whole-group drama about helping others.

†† *Whole class.*

🕐 *Session One: 10 to 15 minutes. Session Two: 20 to 30 minutes.*

Previous skills/knowledge needed

The children should be able to imagine what Santa's toy shop and sleigh might look like.

Key background information

This activity provides a structured opportunity for children to work alongside others in role, and is particularly suitable for very young children. It also adds status to the idea of helping others for no personal gain, other than intrinsic satisfaction. The Christmas theme can be adapted to allow children to help characters from stories. For example, the children may be sent a note asking them to help Jack's mother tidy the garden after the beanstalk fell down. The activity is divided into two sessions. Session One can take place in the classroom, but Session Two needs a large space.

Session One forms an introduction to Session Two, so you will need to restrict the gap between them to being as short as possible.

Preparation

For Session One, make one copy of photocopiable page 147 per child. For Session Two, make one copy of photocopiable page 148 and cut out the two letters from Santa. Place them in separate envelopes and address them both to the children. Put a key in with the letter asking for help. Place the PE mats together to form an oblong shape at the side of the room. They should be large enough for everyone to sit on, including yourself.

Resources needed

Photocopiable pages 147 and 148, drawing and writing materials, a large space (for Session Two), PE mats, sleigh bells or a tambourine, scissors, two envelopes, a door key, a copy of 'Jingle Bells' (*Christmas Carol Time* by F Waterman, Faber Music).

What to do

Session One

Talk about the toys children have for Christmas and how Santa makes some of them in his workshop. Talk briefly about what some simple toys are made of, for example cars made of wood, teddies made of furry material and dolls made of porcelain or plastic. Give each child a copy of photocopiable page 147 and explain what to do, then let everyone complete their sheet.

Session Two

Ask the children to join you in pretending to be in a story about some children and their teacher who helped Santa. Introduce the letter from Santa (photocopiable page 148) containing the key and read it aloud to the children. Show them the letter and talk about it to make sure they understand what they are being asked to do.

Next, ask the class to pretend that the PE mats are the sleigh and explain that later on, they must imagine that the hall is Santa's toy shop. Talk about what the shop might look like, both inside and out. Organize the children to sit with you on the sleigh and remember to take the key and play the sleigh bells. Suggest that everyone sings 'Jingle Bells' until you arrive at the toy shop. Now talk as if you have arrived outside the toy shop and gather the children together to unlock the imaginary door. Use the children's previous ideas about what might be in the shop to describe what you can see, or add some of your own. Ask the children to watch you as you show them where the tools and paint are kept and how to work on the toys.

Choose one category of toy to work on first, such as toys with wheels. Use mime to demonstrate how the children might work on them. Tasks might include painting, fixing wheels, polishing chrome and fixing brakes. Tell the children to work on these toys first and come to you when they have finished. Insist on safety in the shop and discourage children from rushing around. Talk to the children as they work, and find more wheeled toys for those who finish well before the others.

When most of the children have finished, call them together and admire the finished toys. Now select other categories of toys to work on in the same way, such as dolls, teddies, board games and so on. If the children are confident with the mime, there will be no need to demonstrate what to do each time. A brief description of what is required should be sufficient.

Finally, pull out an imaginary box of Christmas wrapping paper and ask the children to wrap some of the smaller toys ready for Santa to put on his sleigh. Then leave the shop and lock the door after you. Climb back on the sleigh and sing 'Jingle Bells' as before, to create the illusion of travelling home. Announce that you have arrived back at school and tell the children to come off the sleigh and sit round you on the floor. Explain that this is the end of the story about some kind children who helped Santa.

Ask the children which parts of the story they liked the best and use this as an opportunity to reflect on the events in the drama. Send the children the second letter from Santa (photocopiable page 148) soon after the drama to thank them for their help.

Suggestion(s) for extension

After each category of toy has been worked on, ask the more confident children to tell the class what they have done to complete the toys. Ask probing questions to encourage them to describe their tasks in detail.

Suggestion(s) for support

Mime working on the toys yourself and ask those who need support to help you. Ask them to follow your instructions or allow them to copy you if necessary.

Assessment opportunities

Note those children who behave appropriately in the dramatic context and those whose verbal contributions show an understanding of the situation. Look for children who can concentrate on the mimed tasks and are able to describe what they are doing when asked.

Opportunities for IT

The children could use an art package to draw pictures of the toys they worked on. They could also use the pictures in a word processor to make a class book of Santa's toys, adding a short sentence to describe the wonderful features of their particular toy. An alternative activity would be to use the pictures in a design of a Christmas card. The children could write and edit a short verse to go inside the card, presenting it in an interesting font.

Performance ideas

Let pairs of children come to the front to perform what they did when they worked on the toys in Santa's shop. Ask the audience to guess what the children are doing.

Display ideas

Let the children draw pictures of the toys they worked on and display these with the second note from Santa thanking the children for their help.

Reference to photocopiable sheets

Photocopiable page 147 focuses on the different parts of toys. This will help the children to visualize working on the toys for the mime in Santa's workshop. Photocopiable page 148 provides the two letters from Santa to add realism to the drama and reward them for their help through Santa's thanks.

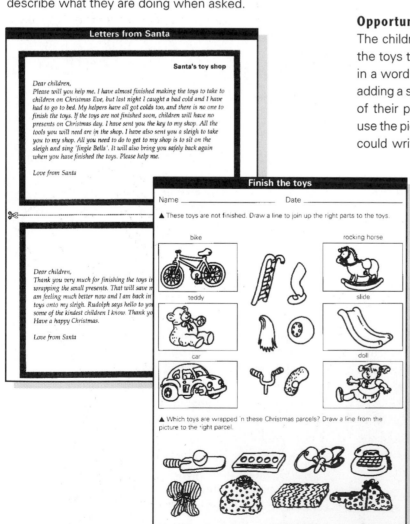

Letters from Santa

Santa's toy shop

Dear children,
Please will you help me. I have almost finished making the toys to take to children on Christmas Eve, but last night I caught a bad cold and I have had to go to bed. My helpers have all got colds too, and there is no one to finish the toys. If the toys are not finished soon, children will have no presents on Christmas day. I have sent you the key to my shop. All the tools you will need are in the shop. I have also sent you a sleigh to take you to my shop. All you need to do to get to my shop is to sit on the sleigh and sing 'Jingle Bells'. It will also bring you safely back again when you have finished the toys. Please help me.

Love from Santa

Dear children,
Thank you very much for finishing the toys in wrapping the small presents. That will save m am feeling much better now and I am back in toys onto my sleigh. Rudolph says hello to yo some of the kindest children I know. Thank yo Have a happy Christmas.

Love from Santa

Finish the toys

Name _____ Date _____

▲ These toys are not finished. Draw a line to join up the right parts to the toys.

bike   rocking horse

teddy   slide

car   doll

▲ Which toys are wrapped in these Christmas parcels? Draw a line from the picture to the right parcel.

PERSONAL ROBOTS

To focus on co-operating with a partner in an imaginary context.

†† *Whole class and pairs.*

🕐 *20 to 30 minutes.*

Previous skills/knowledge needed
The children should understand what a robot is and what a human robot might be like.

Key background information
This activity is designed to encourage trust and co-operation between pairs. It provides a good basis for future pair work involving improvised situations. You will need a hall or similar large space in which to do the activity.

Preparation
Place the PE apparatus at the side of the room.

Resources needed
A large space, small pieces of PE apparatus suitable for use as obstacles.

What to do
Briefly discuss robots and how they move. Now ask the children to imagine how a human robot might move. Ask them to find a space and walk slowly towards you like a human robot, until you say 'Stop'. Tell them that they are robots who are controlled by your voice. Ask them to walk around the room as robots again, starting when you say 'Go forward' and stopping when you say 'Stop', as before. Remind them not to bump into each other.

Next, using the same words for starting and stopping, tell the 'robots' to walk slowly backwards, turning their heads to see where they are going but not their bodies. Follow this by asking them to walk sideways in any direction. Then ask them to walk around the hall again, listening carefully for your commands. Vary the movements using the commands 'Go forwards', 'Go backwards', 'Go sideways' and 'Stop'.

Once the children can follow your simple commands, put them into pairs and ask them to sit at one end of the room with their partners. Place the obstacles around the room and choose one child to be a robot. Set the robot walking by saying 'Go forwards'. Walk beside the robot, using the range of commands to guide it around the obstacles. If you need the robot to move sideways in a specific direction, indicate this by pointing as you command it to go sideways. Tell the robot that if it touches anything, it must stop and wait for you to tell it what to do. Guide the robot to the other side of the room as the children watch. Then ask the child to stop being the robot and join the rest of the class.

DRAMA

Now let pairs of children take turns at being a robot and a guide. The children should guide their robots across the room by walking beside them. They should use the commands and the pointing. Stress that the robots must listen carefully and follow the instructions closely. If you have a large class, limit the congestion by setting off just a few pairs at a time. Ask the pairs to wait for everyone to make the outward journey before changing roles to set off back again. Children who abuse their responsibility by deliberately making their robots walk into obstacles should be withdrawn to watch how others do it before being allowed a second attempt.

Suggestion(s) for extension
Pair up children who understand the terms 'left' and 'right'. Encourage them to use the words 'Go to the left/right' instead of pointing and saying 'Go sideways'. Let confident pairs include more details in their commands such as 'Go forward four small steps'.

Suggestion(s) for support
Let less confident children use the words 'Go round it' when their robot meets an obstacle, instead of using the sideways command.

Assessment opportunities
Look for children who work together well and appear to be sensitive to each other's needs. Also look for children who are sensitive to the needs of the rest of the class. This will be evident where children attempt to prevent their robot from walking into the path of others. This exercise also provides a good opportunity to assess children's sense of direction and their ability to listen carefully and follow instructions.

Opportunities for IT
This activity links well to the control element of work in information technology. The children could be given a small set of commands to use which are similar to those in LOGO control programs (backwards, forwards, turn left, turn right and the number of steps to be taken). Children can work in pairs with this set of instructions to guide each other around the hall or obstacle course. With older pupils one child can be blindfolded to make sure that they cannot make allowances for incorrect instructions.

Children can extend this work using either a floor robot like Roamer or PIPP or a screen turtle program. They can experiment in giving direct commands to the turtle to move it around the screen, make a pattern or explore an obstacle course. The work can then be extended to create a series of linked instructions to guide the floor robot or turtle around a course in one go.

Display ideas
Create a display of model robots made from boxes and art materials. Let each pair of children make one robot between them and invent a suitable name for it which they then attach on a label.

Cross-curricular themes

Drama can be an effective way of teaching many subjects across the whole of the curriculum. Dramatic representations can help young children visualize what life might have been like in the past and this helps them make comparisons with the present. The use of teacher-in-role to reveal historical events is also very effective. Where a teacher teaches about historical events through the eyes of an imagined participant, children relate more closely to the issues and begin to understand some of the implications of those events on people's lives.

Children can learn about weather and environmental issues within a dramatic context through tackling life-like problems as if they were adults. Putting children in roles of responsibility encourages them to think for themselves and form opinions. In this chapter, children are given roles as owners of a popular wildlife centre with a growing litter problem and are asked to consider some solutions.

Aspects of maths can also be approached through drama. In this chapter, physical theatre is the vehicle for encouraging children to represent numbers using their bodies. Whole-group drama is also used to perform mathematical tasks as part of a story. Similarly, aspects of science can be explored effectively through drama. In this chapter, science is taken back to the past, as the children hear about gravity from someone who works on Isaac Newton's farm. Music, too, can be powerfully linked with drama, and in this chapter, the children are encouraged to explore the use of percussion when acting out a story. All in all, there are many rich opportunities for using drama as a powerful cross-curricular teaching tool.

THEN AND NOW

To use freeze-frames to depict and compare aspects of life in the past and present.

Whole class and small groups.

20 to 30 minutes.

Previous skills/knowledge needed

Children need some basic background knowledge in relation to the chosen historical period. For example, to compare a Victorian washday with a modern washday, the children would need to know how the Victorians washed their clothes. Familiarity with the freeze-frame strategy is helpful but not essential.

Key background information

This activity provides a visual focus for comparison and a means of bringing alive aspects of the past which can often seem rather remote or obscure.

The children are invited to make decisions about the depiction of two parallel moments from the past and the present in the form of freeze-frames. Artefacts are used to stimulate discussion and provide a focus for the freeze-frames. Small items of costume can add a touch of realism. Taking photographs helps to raise the status of the activity and provides a resource for further development. The children's photographs can be compared with old photographs or paintings depicting the past.

Preparation

Select an activity as a focus for the freeze-frames. Choose one that will be familiar to the children such as washing clothes, shopping, eating a meal, school playtime or school work. Prepare an acting area large enough for two small groups of children, then set out suitable items of costume for the characters in the freeze-frames. Choose items which are easy to put on and take off, such as scarves, waistcoats, jackets, aprons with Velcro fastenings, shawls and hats. Allocate one item per character but have male and female versions of the same item if possible.

Next, choose one artefact for each freeze-frame, such as a flat iron and a modern steam iron to represent past and present washdays. Props or home-made versions of the historical artefact can be used if authentic artefacts are not available. You may also want to collect old photographs or pictures to help children visualize the activities. Set up the camera and place it nearby.

Resources needed

An acting area, a camera, small items of costume to represent people in the past (see above), clothing to represent the present day (optional), one relevant historical artefact and one modern artefact, drawing materials.

What to do

Sit the children so that everyone can see into the acting area. Use the artefacts to open up a discussion about their

use and make comparisons between the past and the present. Explain that you would like the children to create some imaginary scenes or 'freeze-frames' of the artefacts being used. Make it clear that groups of children will be asked to stand very still as if they were in a picture. Say that you will take photographs of these pictures so that everyone can look at them again.

Now show the children the costumes and discuss which ones should be used for the past and which for the present. Choose one part of the acting area for each freeze-frame and work on them one at a time. Start with whichever one suits the needs of the class. Decide on some appropriate activities first and then choose children who will be the characters performing these. Involve the rest of the class as much as possible in deciding where and how the characters should stand and how they should look. When all the decisions have been made, ask the characters to stand completely still when you say 'Freeze' and to stay like this to the count of five.

Take a photograph of the first freeze-frame before moving on to the second one. After taking a photograph of the second freeze-frame, make the two again simultaneously so the children can see the differences. If possible, take a photograph of the two freeze-frames together. The activity can then be repeated with different children taking up slightly different positions each time. Any differences of opinion in the discussions about the initial freeze-frames can now be accommodated in these subsequent versions.

Finally, ask the children to draw and colour their own versions of the two contrasting moments. They can draw what they remember of the freeze-frames or use their own ideas. Use these pictures later to make comparisons when looking at the photographs of the freeze-frames.

Suggestion(s) for extension
Ask more able children to speculate on what the characters might have been thinking during the moments depicted.

Some children playing the characters may wish to speak their thoughts out loud during the freeze-frame.

Suggestion(s) for support
Differentiate through questioning when discussing the freeze-frames. Give less confident children an opportunity to make some decisions about the details of the freeze-frames, pitched at their level of understanding. Put a less confident child into a frame as one of a pair doing the same activity, such as two people serving on a market stall or two wartime children playing with marbles.

Assessment opportunities
Note those children who are able to express valid points of view about the details of the frames and those who can make appropriate contributions to the discussions. Use the discussions and the pictures to assess how well children understand the differences between the two contrasting moments.

Opportunities for IT
The children could use a word processor to design an information label for one of the artefacts used in the freeze

frames, which could then be displayed as a simple class museum. Older or more able children could add extra information about the artefact.

The children could also write captions for the photographs taken and use these for display purposes. If the photographs can be taken with a digital camera these can be saved to the computer and then added to word processed work. Alternatively if the school has access to a scanner the original photographs can be scanned to make a digital image which can be used in the same way. Using either method the class could make an electronic photograph album.

A more ambitious project would be to combine the text, photographs and children's own voices into a multimedia presentation using authoring software. Each of the freeze frame pictures could be used along with the children's own writing. Their voices can be recorded using a microphone attached to the computer. By clicking on a freeze frame picture the text could be displayed or spoken by the computer. It would even be possible for different characters in the freeze frame to record their own commentary so that by clicking on one of the characters you heard their voice describing aspects of the picture. The presentation could be extended by adding other information relevant to the period being studied.

Performance ideas

Freeze-frames can be brought to life for a few seconds and then frozen again. This will allow the children to mime the actions and talk in role if they wish. These scenes can be rehearsed and made into a series of short performances.

Display ideas

Display the photographs of past moments in paper frames that resemble those of the historical period. Display photographs of the modern moments in frames reflecting today's styles. Invite observers to pick out which freeze-frames depict the past and which depict the present.

SOUNDS LIKE A GOOD STORY

To develop confidence in making sound effects for drama.

†† *Whole class and groups.*

🕐 *30 to 40 minutes.*

Previous skills/knowledge needed

The children should know the main events in the chosen story. They should also be familiar with the sounds of the percussion instruments chosen to accompany the story. Some practice beforehand in using these instruments and a brief discussion of the effects of the different sounds may be helpful.

Key background information

This activity can be adapted to suit whole stories or parts of them. The need to interpret the main events in the story through actions and sound encourages children to look for deeper meanings within the narrative. It also demonstrates how music and sound can be used to complement and enhance a piece of drama.

Preparation

Prepare a space if necessary for movement activities. Select three or four sections from a familiar story which have

potential for sound effects and mime. Most traditional stories have suitable parts, as do sections of more modern stories (see 'Resources' for suggestions). For example, in the story of 'The Elves and The Shoemaker', the first section might involve miming the actions of the shoemaker and his wife as they make what they believe is their last pair of shoes. This could be accompanied by shoemaking sounds using cowbells and triangles. These sounds could be followed by other 'sad' sounds on the instruments, to indicate the feelings of the couple. This can be followed by miming the elves, as they run with tiny steps into the shoemaker's workshop to try on their new clothes, watched by the shoemaker and his wife. Sounds to accompany the elves' light steps can be made using a rainstick or by children making light tapping sounds with their fingers on a tambour. These can be followed by happy sounds made on the instruments. Make a list of the actions and accompanying sounds in each section of your chosen story, and the instruments you need.

Resources needed

A large space, a range of percussion instruments (for example: cowbell, triangle, tambour, rainstick, and so on), a familiar story, either traditional (see above), or modern such as *We're Going On A Bear Hunt*, by Michael Rosen and Helen Oxenbury (Walker) or *Where The Wild Things Are*, by Maurice Sendak (Collins Picture Lions).

What to do

Read the story to the children, explaining that after they have listened to it they will have the chance to act out parts of it. After the story, ask the children to find a space. Choose one of the main characters from the story and say that on the word 'Action' the children must walk around the room as if they were that character. Make it clear that everyone must pretend to be the same character, and that they should walk carefully around without touching one another or talking.

Before starting the activity, talk about how the chosen character might walk or move. Make it clear that the children must listen and react according to your narration. For example, if you say that he/she felt tired and sat down, then the children must stop and sit down. Explain that whenever you say the word 'Freeze', they must stop being the character and sit down. Use this framework to act out the different sections of the story, concentrating on the mimed actions. Let the children make suggestions for these actions before everyone attempts them.

When all the story sections have been acted out, organize the children into one group for each of the sections and set out the percussion instruments. Explain that everyone is now going to concentrate on making the sounds to accompany the story. Let each group be the musicians for a particular section, while the other groups mime the actions. Agree on a visual signal for starting the sounds,

93

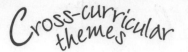

such as a raised hand, and another for stopping, such as a lowered hand. Let groups practise their sounds with these signals before attempting to combine them with the actions to the narration.

Now let the children perform the sections of the story. Orchestrate by using your narration to control the actions and hand signals to control the sounds. Stop between each section to reorganize the groups. Conclude the activity by asking the children which actions and sounds they liked the best and why.

Suggestion(s) for extension
Write out the story in simple language and let confident readers read them aloud for the class. Give a group of more confident children the opportunity to perform all aspects of a section themselves, so that some will act, some will make the sounds and one will read the narration. Encourage them to stop at an agreed point to allow some dialogue between the actors.

Suggestion(s) for support
Give less confident children an opportunity to practise responding to the stopping and starting signals for the sounds before the activity. Talk about the parts of the story to be performed beforehand and ask the children to draw their version of these events.

Assessment opportunities
Note the children's confidence and skill in handling the instruments and their ability to listen to and follow instructions. Observe their mime work for imaginative interpretations of the events and the ability to respond appropriately in role.

Opportunities for IT
Simple elements of control work can be included with the use of a tape recorder to record the music.

Performance ideas
With rehearsal, these sections are particularly suitable for performing to larger audiences. They can be performed in the context of telling the whole story.

KITES AND WASHING

To use whole-group role-play to focus on a geographical theme.
†† *Whole class.*
🕐 *30 minutes.*

Previous skills/knowledge needed
The children should have experienced working alongside each other in a whole-group situation. Some awareness of what windy weather means would be an advantage.

Key background information
This activity provides the children with an imaginary experience where they enjoy aspects of windy weather, but are also confronted with some of the problems it can cause.

Preparation
The children should be taught a simple song or rhyme about the wind such as 'The north wind doth blow'. Make a sign saying 'Red Cottage' and place it on the wall or over the back of a chair at one end of the room. Make one copy per child of photocopiable page 149.

Resources needed
Photocopiable page 149, a large space, writing and drawing materials, a picture showing children flying kites in the wind, a scarf suitable for an elderly person, a piece of card and a felt-tipped pen.

What to do
Introduction: Setting the scene
Sit the children at the side of the hall, opposite the sign saying 'Red Cottage'. Ask if they will join you in pretending to be in a story about some children and their teacher, who went out to fly kites on a cold, windy day. Explain that they

will need to pretend the room is a safe place outside where they can fly their imaginary kites. Point out the sign and say that this is the back door of an imaginary house called 'Red Cottage'. Define the areas of the room that are out of bounds.

Now show the picture of children flying kites and ask what special clothing is needed for a cold and windy day. Invite the children to copy you as you mime putting on the clothes. Then ask them to think about the colour of the imaginary kites they are going to fly. Tell them to fold their arms when they have chosen a colour. When everyone has decided, call out the names of some colours and ask the children to put up their hands when you say their colour. Using mime, suggest that the children pack their kites carefully into their imaginary bags.

Development
Announce that you are ready to start the story. Using a narrative style, start the story as follows:
Once upon a time, a group of children and their teacher went out on a cold, windy day and this is what happened... From this point, behave as if the events are really happening. Ask the children to stand with you in a group. Explain that the wind is so strong that you will not be able to walk very quickly. Warn everyone to hold on tightly to their bags.

Now organize the children into a crocodile formation and tell them to follow you as you set off walking. Talk about how the trees are swaying and say that you are looking for an open space where the kites will not become caught up in the trees. Remember to walk with difficulty due to the

wind. Move in a circular direction around the room for a short time and then stop to announce that you have come to a tree blown down by the wind. Remark on how dangerous this could be and lead the children over it very carefully. Eventually announce that you have found a nice open space to fly the kites.

Tell the children to sit down and take their kites carefully out of their bags (mime this along with them). Demonstrate how to launch a kite and talk about how to fly and control it. Now invite the children to fly theirs. After a while, direct putting the kites away and suggest that you all sing a song or say a rhyme about the wind before you go home (see 'Preparation').

After the song, tell the children that you will now act out what happens next in the story. Resume the narrative tone and explain that an elderly person came out of Red Cottage looking very sad, and wanted to talk to the children. Say that you will pretend to be that person when you put on the scarf. Take on the role of the elderly person and explain the following problem: You thought that a windy day was a good day to dry your washing but the wind is so strong it has blown your washing off the line and into the bushes. The bushes are very big and you can't reach your washing. To make matters worse, you have left your warm coat at your friend's house. You can't go into the garden without your coat as you have not been well.

Still in role, ask the children if they will help you, but emphasize that they will not be able to reach the washing easily, as it has blown far into the bushes. Ask them for

DRAMA

again and lead them back through the trees. Tell them that the broken tree has now been moved to let the traffic pass. Lead everyone back to the side of the room where they began and announce that this is the end of the story.

Conclusion

Ask children to share their favourite parts of the story with the rest of the class. Praise everyone for helping the elderly person and talk about the problems caused by windy weather in real life. Move to the classroom and conclude the activity by asking each child to complete photocopiable page 149.

Suggestion(s) for extension

Before starting the story, ask the more confident children to demonstrate walking in the strong wind. Tell them to hold onto their bags as they walk. Encourage them to lean forward and walk slowly as if they were pushing against something. When you reach the fallen tree, ask a more confident child to report it to the police using your imaginary mobile phone.

suggestions on how they might overcome this problem. If they suggest using equipment, point to a shed where it can be found. Stress that everyone must move slowly and carefully, so as not to drop the washing or hurt themselves.

Before the children start, indicate exactly where the bushes are and ask everyone to put the washing in the shed when they have reached it. Allow the class time to complete the task. If any children behave inappropriately, stay in role but call them back and remind them of your safety concerns. After they have finished, thank everyone for their help.

Stay in role as the elderly person and announce that your fence has blown down in the wind. Ask the children if they will help you to fix it. Show them where it is broken and demonstrate how to fetch hammers and nails from your shed in order to fix the fence. Give the children a few minutes to complete this task, then thank them again for their help and ask them to sing you a song or a rhyme about the wind to cheer you up before they go. Say goodbye and take off the scarf to come out of role.

Now organize the children into a crocodile formation

Suggestion(s) for support

Let the children look at a real kite before the drama activity. Encourage less confident children to stay near you during the drama. Ask them to help you with special jobs, such as folding the washing as the other children bring it into the shed, or holding bags of nails for the children fixing the fence.

Assessment opportunities

The drama provides an opportunity to assess the children's ability to respond appropriately in role and reflect upon their experiences when out of role. Children can also be assessed on their confidence in speaking and listening within a whole-group situation.

Opportunities for IT

The children could use an art or drawing package to design their own kites. They could experiment to create different patterns to decorate the kites. They may need to be shown how to create different shapes and fill them with colours.

Display ideas

Cut out and glue the children's drawings of the washing (on their photocopiable sheet) onto pieces of plain paper. Secure a washing line against a wall or across the room and peg the papers onto the line. Copy out the song or rhyme about the wind and display it near the washing line. The children can also make drawings or paintings of their imaginary kites to add to the display.

Reference to photocopiable sheet

Photocopiable page 149 encourages the children to reflect on their experience of the drama.

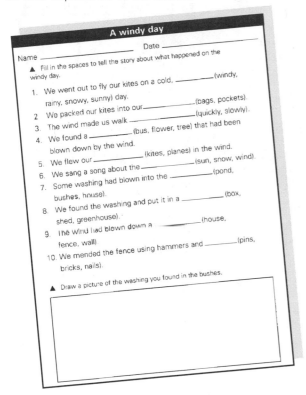

A windy day

Name _____ Date _____

▲ Fill in the spaces to tell the story about what happened on the windy day.

1. We went out to fly our kites on a cold, _____ (windy, rainy, snowy, sunny) day.
2. We packed our kites into our _____ (bags, pockets).
3. The wind made us walk _____ (quickly, slowly).
4. We found a _____ (bus, flower, tree) that had been blown down by the wind.
5. We flew our _____ (kites, planes) in the wind.
6. We sang a song about the _____ (sun, snow, wind).
7. Some washing had blown into the _____ (pond, bushes, house).
8. We found the washing and put it in a _____ (box, shed, greenhouse).
9. The wind had blown down a _____ (house, fence, wall).
10. We mended the fence using hammers and _____ (pins, bricks, nails).

▲ Draw a picture of the washing you found in the bushes.

JEAN'S WAR

To use teacher-in-role to stimulate role play on a historical theme.

†† *Whole class and small groups.*

🕐 *Session One: 20 to 30 minutes. Session Two: 30 to 45 minutes.*

Previous skills/knowledge needed

The children will need some simple background knowledge about life in a British city during the Second World War. Some familiarity with wartime games such as hopscotch, marbles and skipping to rhymes would be helpful. Some experience of freeze-frames would also be an advantage (see 'Special moments' on page 14).

Key background information

Teaching history through role-play lends a personal perspective to events which can otherwise be difficult for children to grasp. Session One allows children to view aspects of the war through the eyes of a twelve-year-old child. It focuses on games and songs to balance the negative aspects of the war revealed during the role play. Session Two involves the children in taking on roles as evacuees.

Session One provides a model for the children's role play in Session Two, and so the gap between the sessions should be no longer than a week. Use the words 'Action' and 'Freeze' to start and stop the drama each time. Blow the whistle before you say 'Freeze', if necessary.

Preparation

Make one copy per child of photocopiable page 150 for Session One, and one copy per child of photocopiable page 151 for Session Two.

Resources needed

Photocopiable pages 150 and 151, a large space, a plain cardigan or school tie suitable for the teacher to wear when in role as a twelve-year-old child during the Second World War, a traditional action song that might have been sung by wartime children, such as 'Oranges and Lemons' or 'Farmer's in his Den' in *Oranges and Lemons* by Ian Beck and Karen King (Oxford University Press), two traditional nursery rhymes that the children know well, a whistle.

What to do

Session One

Talk briefly about what life was like for children in British cities during the Second World War. Tell the children that when you put on the cardigan and/or tie, you will pretend to be a twelve-year-old child who lived during the war. Ask them to listen carefully to the child to see what they can find out about the war.

Put on the clothing and tell the children that your name is Jean (or Jim), and that you have younger brothers and sisters to look after. Talk about how your dad has gone to war and how your mum works in a nursery. Explain that many women in your town have to work in factories. They have to help make weapons for the war and so they can't look after their babies in the daytime. The babies therefore go to a nursery during the day and your mum helps to look after them.

Ask the children if they would like to play a game that you play with your brothers and sisters. Teach them an action song (see 'Resources'), then talk about other things you like to play, such as skipping, marbles and hopscotch. Ask if the children ever play these games, and mention others that are popular such as football and cricket.

After the discussion, sit the children around you and tell them that you are tired. Talk about the nightly air raids and how you have to take your brothers and sisters down into the air raid shelter. Describe how frightened you all are and how cramped it is down in the shelter. Talk about the night when you refused to go down there and how the house next door was bombed. Explain that some children have been sent away from their homes to stay in the countryside where there is no bombing.

Move on to tell the children about how you try to cheer up your brothers and sisters in the shelter by singing nursery rhymes. Ask them if they will sing some with you to cheer you up. Sing one or two rhymes together and look visibly more cheerful, thanking the children for cheering you up. Explain that you now have to go and get the ration book, so that you can go shopping. Talk about the restrictions on sugar, sweets and other food before leaving.

Turn your back to the class and take off the clothing to come out of role. Make it clear that you are now back to being yourself. Ask the children what they have found out about life during the war and encourage them to make comparisons with life today. Ask each child to complete a copy of photocopiable page 150 back in the classroom. This will help to reinforce their knowledge in preparation for Session Two.

Session Two

Put the children into groups of three or four. Ask them to pretend to be a group of Jean's friends who lived during the war and to imagine that the room is the school playground. Explain that the playground is very small because last week part of it was bombed and now cannot be used. Ask the children to think of some wartime games that they could play in a small playground. Make it clear that games involving running around, such as tig, football and cricket are not suitable in the small playground.

Now discuss some possibilities for games, such as hop scotch, marbles, skipping and playing with small balls. Explain that these games will need to be mimed and ask the children to demonstrate. Then let them decide in their groups on two games they will play in the playground. Ask them to choose which one they will play first and then fold their arms to show they have decided. Make it clear that the children will need to talk to each other in the playground as if it were wartime. Talk about what they might say to each other. This might involve organizing the games or talking about the bombing.

Explain that the drama will start as if the children are frozen in an old photograph. Talk about how they might be positioned and ask volunteers to demonstrate. Then give the groups a few seconds to decide on their photograph positions. Say that when everyone is frozen, you will say 'Action' to bring the photograph to life. They must then play their games until you stop the drama.

Send groups into the playground area, a few at a time, to stand in the freeze position. Encourage the first groups to keep still as they wait for the other groups to join them. Start the drama and let the playground come alive for several minutes or until the children lose concentration. Then freeze the action and ask the children to sit at the side of the room.

Announce that you will play the part of Jean again when you put on the clothing as before. In role as Jean, tell the children that everyone in the school is to be evacuated next week. Explain what this means and tell them that you have mixed feelings about the idea. Talk about

the positive side, in that you will be safe from the bombs and living in pleasant countryside. Then talk about having to leave your family and the fear that your house might be bombed while you are away.

Move on to discuss your fears about living with strangers who may give you food you don't like or perhaps even be unkind. Make it clear that your family will not be able to contact you except by letter, because of the lack of telephones and transport. Tell the children that everyone will only be allowed to take one small bag and so they should choose what they put in it with care. Then take off the clothing to come out of role.

Now discuss the kinds of things the children could pack in their small bags to remind them of home. Give the class a few seconds to think about what they will pack and tell them to fold their arms when they have decided. Encourage them to think about this on their own. When most have decided, ask them to imagine that a corner of the room is their bedroom. Demonstrate how to mime taking a small bag from a cupboard and packing it with clothes and the things they have chosen to remind them of home. Explain that in a moment, you will ask everyone to find their own space for their bedroom and they should then pack their bags on their own.

Before the children begin, indicate an area of the room to represent the railway station where they will catch the train to be evacuated. Tell them to walk to this area after they have packed their bags and stand as if they are waiting for the train. Explain that when they reach the station, they should tell their friends what they have put in their bags. Start the drama, then stop it again when all the children have packed their bags and reached the station.

Tell the children to sit down in the station area. Ask them how they feel about being evacuated. Talk about what they might think about on the train, then say that you will tell them what happened at the end of the story. Explain that the children went on the train and were met on arrival by some village people. Say

that some of these people were kind to the children but some were not. Many children were homesick and went home, some ran away and some stayed and had a lovely time. At the end of the war, all the children went home. Conclude the activity by asking each child to fill in a copy of photocopiable page 151, working with a partner.

Suggestion(s) for extension
In Session One, add more details about life during the war, such as the blackouts and references to the fighting, for the more able children. Ask these children more detailed questions during the final discussion. In Session Two, let the children perform their games and conversations in the playground to the rest of the class before you re-introduce Jean. When talking about their feelings at the station, ask more able children to tell you what they were thinking, using the first person as in a thought bubble.

Suggestion(s) for support
For less able children, keep Jean's language simple and the anecdotes colloquial in Session One. This should help to keep the children's attention. During the final discussion,

differentiate through questions. This might involve asking direct recall questions about the game and the songs, or questions about how Joan felt during the bombing. In Session Two, put less confident children together in a group and support them by joining in the activities with them as Jean.

Assessment opportunities
Note those children who listen well to Jean's stories and can recall the main points. Note also any children who are able to make comparisons between life in the war and life today. Look for children who respond appropriately and sensitively in the role of evacuee.

Opportunities for IT
The children could use an encyclopaedia CD-ROM to search for information about life during the war. They will need to be shown how to set up a simple search and to use the highlighted 'hyperlinks' in the text that will take them to related information. They may want to print out the relevant information once they have found it. They could also search for other aspects of the activity such as nursery rhymes

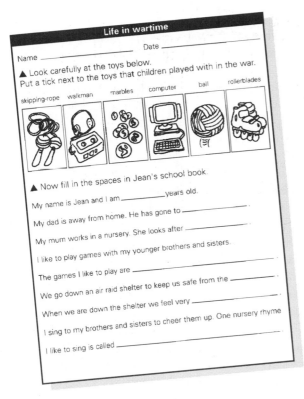

Life in wartime

Name _____ Date _____

▲ Look carefully at the toys below.
Put a tick next to the toys that children played with in the war.

skipping-rope   walkman   marbles   computer   ball   rollerblades

▲ Now fill in the spaces in Jean's school book.

My name is Jean and I am _____ years old.

My dad is away from home. He has gone to _____

My mum works in a nursery. She looks after _____

I like to play games with my younger brothers and sisters.

The games I like to play are _____

We go down an air raid shelter to keep us safe from the _____ .

When we are down the shelter we feel very _____

I sing to my brothers and sisters to cheer them up. One nursery rhyme

I like to sing is called _____

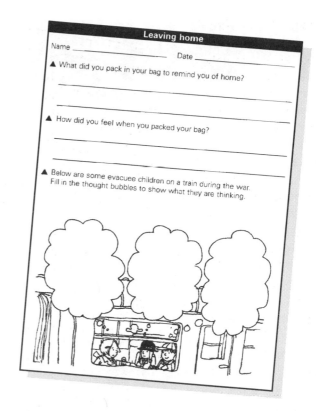

Leaving home

Name _____ Date _____

▲ What did you pack in your bag to remind you of home?

▲ How did you feel when you packed your bag?

▲ Below are some evacuee children on a train during the war.
Fill in the thought bubbles to show what they are thinking.

and children's games. The children could combine the information they have found with suitable pictures which could be taken from the CD-ROM or specific CD-ROM collections.

The children could also use a word processor to create their own list of items that they would pack in their suitcase if they were being evacuated. These could be presented for a display on the wall or combined to make a class book. Children could also add simple illustrations created using an art package or taken from collections of suitable clip art.

Display ideas
Collect some everyday wartime artefacts and pictures and display these alongside the children's drawings of Jean's experiences. Draw an outline of bags used by the evacuees and paste inside children's drawings of the things they packed to remind them of home. Some children may also like to contribute poems about their feelings as evacuees. Give the display a title such as 'Bags of memories'.

Reference to photocopiable sheets
Photocopiable page 150 helps to reinforce the information gained in Session One, which will help the children take on the roles of wartime children in Session Two. Photocopiable page 151 acts as a conclusion to the drama and invites the children to reflect on the thoughts and feelings they experienced as prospective evacuees.

SHEPHERDS, ANGELS, AND A STAR

> ***To perform a dance drama on a religious theme.***
> 👥 *Whole class.*
> 🕐 *30 to 40 minutes.*

Previous skills/knowledge needed

Children need to be familiar with the main events in the Christmas story and should be able to work alongside each other in a movement situation.

Key background information

This activity explores and reinforces part of the Christmas story through movement and dance. The movements portray the sequence of events surrounding the shepherds' discovery of baby Jesus in the stable.

Preparation

Talk to the children about the religious meaning of Christmas and focus on the part of the Christmas story in which the angels appear to the shepherds. Make one copy of photocopiable page 152 per child. Draw an outline of a star on a sheet of stiff paper or card. Make sure the children are dressed in a PE kit or similar suitable clothing.

Resources needed

Photocopiable page 152, a large space, a sheet of stiff paper or card, a felt-tipped pen, a doll to represent the baby Jesus, a tambourine, a tambour, finger bells or similar.

What to do

Introduction: Making stars

Discuss with the children how a bright star shone over the stable where Jesus was born, and hold up the star outline. Talk about its pointed shape and ask the children to make star shapes with their hands by spreading their fingers wide. Then ask if they can put both their hands together to make another star shape with hands touching at the wrists. Then tell them to make their stars slowly disappear into fist shapes. Ask them to repeat this to make stars appear and disappear.

Now ask the children to find a space and let them make a larger star shape with their whole bodies. Encourage them to try different ways of doing this, such as balancing on

one leg or using different levels on their knees. Let them show their different versions to the class. Then ask them to work out how to move from a crouched position into their star shapes and let one or two children demonstrate their ideas. Finally, ask everyone to crouch down and then move into their star shapes as you shake the tambourine.

Moving like angels
Discuss the moment when the angels came to tell the shepherds about the birth of Jesus. Talk about how angels are depicted with their arms and wings outstretched or folded. Let the children try slowly opening and closing their arms like folding and unfolding wings. Talk about how angels are sometimes depicted kneeling, and ask everyone to kneel down slowly like angels, opening and closing their arms as though they were wings.

Next, ask the children to walk around the room like angels, again opening and closing their wings. They should stop every so often to kneel, as before. Use the finger bells to accompany the angel movements. When the children have mastered this, let them perform their angels to each other, half the class at a time.

The shepherds
Discuss how the shepherds were watching their sheep at night before the angel Gabriel appeared. Talk about how the shepherds might have been sitting or standing by an open fire, warming their hands or just watching the sheep in the fields. Mention how some shepherds might have been lying down to rest or walking slowly around to check

on the sheep. Now ask the children to move like the shepherds, sometimes walking and looking, sometimes sitting and warming hands, and sometimes lying down.

Encourage them to move slowly from one movement to another and to use as many different positions as possible. Accompany the shepherd movements using a repeated rhythm of two rapid beats followed by a pause and then another beat on the tambour. Let the children perform their movements to each other half the class at a time.

Development: Making a dance drama
Organize the shepherd, angel and star movements into a sequence with the accompanying percussion instruments. Start with the shepherds and finish with the star. Use the instruments to signal when to change from one movement to another. Let the class perform this as a whole group, followed by a performance from half the class at a time.

Adding a narrative
Choose three children to represent the nativity scene group of Mary and Joseph and the star. Choose a few children to represent the group of angels and ask the rest of the class to represent the group of shepherds. Organize the shepherd group to sit in one part of the room and the angel group to sit in an adjacent area. Position the nativity group as far away as possible from the other two groups and ask Mary and Joseph to sit on the floor, in front of the star. Let Mary hold the doll to represent Jesus.

Now organize the following sequence, with yourself as the narrator:

> *(The children sit on the floor in their designated areas.)*
>
> **Narrator:** One night, a long time ago in Bethlehem, some shepherds were watching their sheep on the hillside...
>
> *(The shepherds perform their movements to the tambour and sit down on one final loud beat.)*
>
> **Narrator:** When suddenly, some angels appeared.
>
> *(The angels perform their movements to the finger bells. The shepherds watch the angels.)*
>
> **Narrator:** The angels told the shepherds that Jesus had been born in a stable. They pointed to a bright star.
>
> *(The angels point to the star and the shepherds look at this. The child representing the star makes the shape behind Mary and Joseph.)*
>
> **Narrator:** The angels told the shepherds that they would find the baby Jesus under the star. The shepherds left their sheep and walked towards the star.
>
> *(The shepherds slowly walk to sit in front of Mary and Joseph, followed by the angels who stand with wings unfolded at either side of the star.)*
>
> **Narrator:** The shepherds found Mary and Joseph with the baby Jesus in a stable.

After running through the sequence once, discuss how each group might have felt; for example, the shepherds were surprised and scared; the angels were happy, Mary and Joseph were pleased but surprised to see the shepherds. Ask various children to demonstrate how they might express these feelings in their faces. Suggest that the child playing the star move his or her fingers to indicate twinkling. Then run through the sequence again, perhaps finishing with a familiar carol such as 'While Shepherds Watched' or 'Away in a Manger'.

Conclusion

Conclude the activity by asking each child to complete a copy of photocopiable page 152. Briefly discuss what the people in the nativity scene (in the stable) might have been thinking, then include the whole class in a final tableau of the moment with appropriate expressions.

Suggestion(s) for extension

After completing the photocopiable sheet, ask a small group or groups of the more confident children to prepare two tableaux based on the pictures and ask them to say their own versions of the people's thoughts out loud, as they stand in the tableaux. These can be performed to the rest of the class.

Suggestion(s) for support

Arrange for children needing support to look at pictures of the Christmas story prior to the drama. Ask them to talk about and draw the moment when the angels appeared to the shepherds. Pair less confident children with more confident partners during the movement activities and let them work in a group to help them fill in their photocopiable sheet.

Assessment opportunities

Look for children who can use their bodies and faces appropriately to express the movements and feelings within the story. Note those children who are able to remember instructions and respond appropriately when performing the final movement sequence.

Opportunities for IT

The children could use a word processor to write and present their thought bubble for the class display. A thought bubble shape could be set up as a template for them to use, or they could format their text into a bubble shape and then cut it out once they have printed it. The children will need to know how to format their text using the return key to break up lines into shorter lengths, or the delete key to join them up again to fit inside the bubble shape. They will also need to be able to change the size of the font to fit the bubble and to ensure the text can be read from a distance.

Performance ideas

With a little rehearsal, the final movement sequence of this activity can be made into a simple whole-class performance for a wider audience.

Display ideas

Ask each child to paint or draw the figure they represented in the final movement activity and include the star. The children should cut out their figures and paste them onto a large sheet to make a nativity picture for display. Leave space above each figure to draw in a thought bubble. Ask some or all of the children to write a thought for their figure on the picture. The child who played the star can help another child write a thought for their figure.

Reference to photocopiable sheet

Photocopiable sheet 152 encourages the children to consider the thoughts of Mary, Joseph, and the angels and shepherds. It also encourages the children to make a more thoughtful version of the final tableau.

WILDLIFE PARK

To give children an opportunity to take on roles of responsibility within a dramatic context.

†† *Whole class and small groups.*

⏻ *Session One: 30 to 45 minutes. Session Two: 45 minutes.*

Previous skills/knowledge needed

The children should have some knowledge of what a wildlife park is and the kind of animals or creatures found there.

Key background knowledge

This activity works best where children have been on a visit to a wildlife park, or are studying a related topic. The activity stands on its own, but it does have potential as a stimulus for map making and extended writing (see display ideas). There are two sessions; Session One can be completed in the classroom, but Session Two requires a large space.

Session One forms an introduction to Session Two and so the time in-between should be no more than a week. The jobs undertaken by the children at the start of Session Two work to build belief in the drama and encourage commitment to the wildlife park. This helps to motivate children to discuss and solve the litter problem later in the activity.

DRAMA

Preparation

For Session One, make one copy per child of photocopiable page 153. Make a large sketch map similar to the one shown below and place this in the classroom where everyone can see it. Fold about a dozen sheets of A4 card in half. For Session Two, place the sketch map on a small movable easel or board. Place two large blue PE mats lengthways across the hall to represent part of the river. Write a letter using the following as a guide.

Dear workers

I visited your wildlife park yesterday and I was pleased to see how well you look after the creatures. However, I was not so pleased about the rubbish that I saw all over the park. Your park is a very nice place to visit, but it is very untidy. People are dropping litter all over the place and it could be dangerous. The papers could catch fire and if the animals were to eat the rubbish they could die. Please put some bins in the park and put up some signs to stop people dropping litter. Thank you.

Yours truly

Mrs Exley

Resources needed

Photocopiable page 153, information on creatures likely to be found in a wildlife park (books and publicity leaflets), a large sheet of white paper and felt-tipped pens (for the sketch map), a letter to the wildlife park (see 'Preparation'), a dozen sheets of white A4 card, writing materials, a large space (for Session Two), two large blue PE mats and a whistle.

What to do

Session One

Show the children the sketch map (see above) and explain that it represents a new wildlife park. Ask them to decide what creatures they would like to see in the park. Organize the children into groups of three and decide on about ten to twelve different animals, according to the number of groups. Ask various children to decide where these creatures should be located on the map. Mark the locations by drawing small pictures or symbols to represent each creature on the map.

Allocate a group of children to each creature and ask them to write the name of their creature on a sheet of A4 card. Ask groups to imagine that they are people who look after the creatures at the park. Now give each child a copy of photocopiable page 153 and explain that they need to fill this in as an information sheet about their creature and how they look after it. Give them access to appropriate sources of information in order to complete the sheets. Explain that group members can help each other, but everyone should fill in one sheet each.

Session Two

Place the sketch map in the hall. Ask the children to pretend that the hall is the wildlife park, then define the areas to be used in the drama. Explain that the PE mats represent the part of the river between the bridge and the stepping stones. Let the children refer to the map to decide where their creatures would be located in the room and let groups take turns to put their signs in the correct places on the floor. Each group should then sit behind the sign for their creature(s).

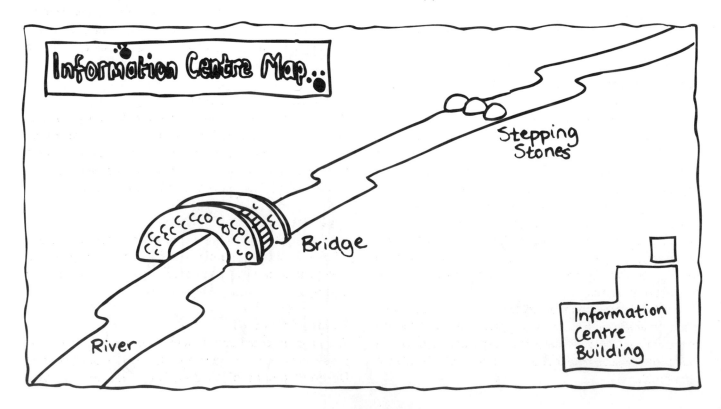

Ask the children if they will pretend to be the workers who look after their creatures. Explain that when you bring the park to life they must mime their jobs, finishing one before they start another. Give groups a few minutes to decide on what jobs they will do and tell them to fold their arms when they have done so. Make it clear that they will be allowed to talk to each other in role as they work.

Tell the children that when you say the word 'Action', the park will come to life as the workers carry out their jobs, but when you blow the whistle and say 'Freeze', they must stop. Bring the park to life and observe the children carefully. Continue for as long as most children seem to be engaged in the activity, then freeze the action and gather everyone together in the area that represents the information centre.

Now ask the children to pretend to be the workers at an important meeting. Tell them that you will pretend to be one of the people who works in the information centre. In role as this person, explain that the park has received a letter of complaint. Read out the letter (see 'Preparation') and ask the children if they will mime making some bins and signs. Talk about what colour and size the bins should be and ask the children to give reasons for their opinions. Talk about the signs and whether they should be polite signs, direct instructions not to drop litter, or threats carrying fines. If they cannot reach an agreement, then ask each person to make up their own mind about what they prefer.

Tell the children that they will find everything they need to make the bins and signs in the sheds around the park. Talk briefly about what they will need to make the bins, for example some wood and nails. Ask them to mime making one bin and one sign each and to put them where they think they are most needed. When most children have attempted this activity, freeze the action and call them back together. Talk about where they decided to place the bins and signs and why they chose these locations.

Finally, ask the groups to practise acting out a short scene showing visitors looking at some of the creatures, having a picnic and putting their rubbish in the bins after reading the signs. Then invite some groups to perform their scenes to the rest of the class.

Tell the children that the park has become a much tidier place because of their work and explain that this is the end of the drama. Talk about real wildlife parks and other leisure parks, and discuss how these places attempt to solve the litter problem.

Suggestion(s) for extension

Encourage the more able children to research and write about their creatures in more detail on the photocopiable sheet in Session One. In preparation for Session Two, these children use simple items to create some of the sounds that the creatures might make first thing in the morning before the workers arrive. Encourage them to think of subtle sounds, such as rustling noises as small creatures scurry through the leaves. These can be used to start the drama just before the workers begin their jobs.

Suggestion(s) for support

Put less confident children into mixed-ability groups for both sessions. In Session Two, take on the role of a park supervisor, and ask children who need individual support to help you carry out general tasks at the park, such as repairing the bridge or unloading a truck of animal food.

Assessment opportunities

Look for children who respond appropriately in role and who contribute to the discussions in a meaningful way. Note any children who are able to give reasons for their opinions.

Opportunities for IT

The children could use a word processor to create and present the signs to go up in the park about the litter. Different groups of children could design their own message which can be displayed in the classroom. The children could also extend the activity by using an art or drawing package to design posters advertising the park. These could contain pictures of animals drawn by the children or taken from clip art collections.

Display ideas
Make and display some items for a park information centre. These could include a 3D model of the park, the children's information sheets about the creatures, route maps on how to find different creatures or pictures of animals on sale as posters, postcards or jigsaw puzzles.

Reference to photocopiable sheet
Photocopiable page 153 encourages the children to think about the creatures they will be responsible for in the drama and requires them to consider the jobs necessary to care for the creatures.

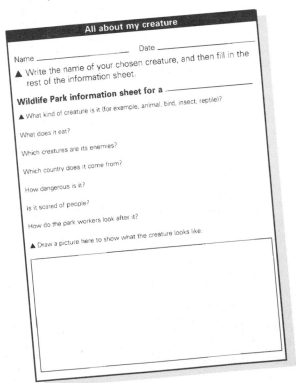

All about my creature

Name _____ Date _____
▲ Write the name of your chosen creature, and then fill in the rest of the information sheet.

Wildlife Park information sheet for a _____
▲ What kind of creature is it (for example, animal, bird, insect, reptile)?

What does it eat?

Which creatures are its enemies?

Which country does it come from?

How dangerous is it?

Is it scared of people?

How do the park workers look after it?

▲ Draw a picture here to show what the creature looks like.

💻 **HEALTHY LIVING**

To use whole-group drama as a way of enabling children to express their understanding of health issues.

†† *Whole class and pairs.*

🕐 *30 to 45 minutes.*

Previous skills/knowledge needed
The children need a basic understanding of healthy foods and what constitutes a healthy lifestyle for children. They should know the rhyme 'There was an Old Woman who Lived in a Shoe'.

Key background information
This activity focuses on putting children into the role of experts who know more than the character played by the teacher. This stimulates language and encourages the children to apply what they know to a different situation.

Preparation
Make one copy of photocopiable page 154 per child. Make one sign saying 'Supermarket' and another saying 'Shoe House'. Place the 'Shoe House' sign on the wall or on a

chair on one side of the room and the 'Supermarket' sign on the opposite side. Place the scarf near the 'Shoe House' sign.

Resources needed
Photocopiable page 154, a large space, writing materials (pencils), two sheets of card, a felt-tipped pen, an adult's scarf.

What to do
Introduction: Thinking about healthy food
Talk about which foods are good for people and which foods should be eaten in moderation. Put the children in pairs, then give out one copy of photocopiable page 154 to each child and ask them to complete the activities. The last part involves working with a partner. Once the children have finished this, let a few pairs show their role-plays to the class or let each pair perform a few at a time.

Development: Setting the scene
Point to the 'Supermarket' and 'Shoe House' signs and ask the children to pretend that these are hanging outside the places they name. Make the connection between the rhyme about the 'Old Woman who lived in a shoe' and 'Shoe House'. Invite them to pretend to be in a story about visiting the Old Woman who lived in the shoe to help her out with all her children. Define the area of the hall to be used. Just before the drama starts, explain that when the children arrive at 'Shoe House', all the bedroom curtains are closed. Someone comes to the door, but it isn't the Old Woman.

Tell the children that when you put on the scarf, you will pretend to be the person who opened the door. Then put on the scarf and play the role of the Old Woman's friend. Explain that the Old Woman has left you to look after her children while she takes a short holiday. Then describe the following problem: *The bedroom curtains are closed because all the children are ill in bed and some of them are asleep. You called the doctor and he said that the children are ill because they are not eating healthy food. All the children have been eating for their dinners is chocolates, sweets, ice cream and crisps. You have looked in the kitchen and there is no more food except some chocolate. The doctor said that you should go to the supermarket and fetch the children some healthy food, but you are not sure what to buy.*

Say that you can't go to the supermarket anyway because you have promised the Old Woman that you will not leave the children.

Now ask the children if they will go to the supermarket for you. Ask them to tell you what they will buy. Warn them not to rush

around in the supermarket, and emphasize that they should carry the food back carefully. Point in the direction of the supermarket sign and quickly give them some imaginary money each before they go. The children should go off to the supermarket and repeat a similar shopping mime to the one practised earlier using the photocopiable sheet. While they do this, move to another part of the room as if you are in the kitchen and, as the children return, ask them to put the food away in the kitchen cupboards (indicate where these are by opening imaginary cupboard doors).

Now gather the children in the kitchen area and thank them for doing your shopping. Enquire about whether they were able to buy what they wanted, then ask if they will help you to cook the children's tea using the healthy food. Talk about some possible menus and show the children where they can work. When most children have finished miming their cooking activities, call them together and thank them for their help again.

Move on to discuss the fact that the Old Woman never lets the children play in the garden. Ask them if they think it's important for children to play in a safe place in the fresh air. Question them about what games you can organize and what toys you can give the Old Woman's children to keep them healthy. Encourage the children to suggest one or two games involving exercise, then thank them for their advice and take off the scarf to come out of role.

Conclusion
Talk about what everyone made for the children's tea and relate this to their own eating habits. Point out that it is

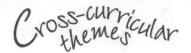
acceptable to eat chocolates, sweets and crisps and so on in small amounts. Ask the children to recall the advice they gave about games and activities and reinforce the message about the need for exercise.

Suggestion(s) for extension
Ask more able children to provide details about how they made the meals in the kitchen. After the drama, let confident writers write out a suggested weekly shopping list for the Old Woman.

Suggestion(s) for support
Ask less confident children to buy just one or two specific items at the imaginary supermarket and let them tell you what they intend to buy before they go. Support some children by asking them to help you make a particular meal in the kitchen.

Assessment opportunities
Look for children who can adapt their knowledge of healthy food to the needs of the imaginary situation. Note those children who can express appropriate ideas clearly and with confidence and those who make appropriate responses in mime.

Opportunities for IT
The children could use a word processor to write out instructions for the menu or for a game that the children can play in the garden. In each case they should look at some examples of the menus or instructions to see the kind of language used and how they are presented. Children

might need to know how to make the titles of the sections of their work stand out, by adding bold text or underlining it. They may also need to number the instructions. Suitable pictures could be added to make their work more interesting to look at.

Display ideas
Let the children draw pictures of the healthy meals they made and glue these onto paper plates for a display. Add any related written work, such as menus or shopping lists for the Old Woman and a copy of the nursery rhyme.

Reference to photocopiable sheet
Photocopiable page 154 prepares children for the whole-group drama by asking them to identify healthy food and practise acting out shopping for this.

THE GARDEN OF SHAPES

To use whole-group drama as a context for mathematical tasks.

†† *Individual work, whole class and pairs.*

🕐 *Session One: 30 minutes. Session Two: 20 to 30 minutes.*

Previous skills/knowledge needed

Children need experience of playing with cubes, cuboids, spheres and cylinders. They should also be familiar with the terms 'curves', 'cubes' and 'cuboids' and be told the names for 'sphere' and 'cylinder'.

Key background information

This activity involves children in carrying out mathematical tasks within the context of a dramatized story. Take the opportunity to ask probing questions about shape whenever possible. Session One can take place in the classroom, but Session Two needs a large space. Session Two should follow as soon after Session One as possible.

Preparation

For Session One, make one copy of photocopiable page 155 per child. Write out an advert, using the one below as a guide, to read out to the children. For Session Two, make a sign saying 'Cubes and cuboids' and a sign saying 'Curves' and place them on the floor on opposite sides of the room. Collect a mixture of plastic and/or wooden 3D shapes, plus a few cardboard boxes (see below). Cover any writing on the shapes or boxes with coloured paper. Mix these up and arrange them in an untidy pile in the middle of the room. Set up a camera with enough film to take two photographs.

Resources needed

Photocopiable page 155, drawing materials, the advert (see 'Preparation') a large space (for Session Two), a camera, a gardener's jacket to fit an adult, two sheets of A4 card, a felt-tipped pen, a collection of cubes, cuboids, spheres and cylinders of different sizes and colours, at least two of each shape, with enough in total for half the number of children in the class.

What to do

Session One

Begin by talking about 3D shapes and showing the children some examples of cubes, cuboids, cylinders and spheres. Include the term 'curves' when talking about cylinders and spheres. Then give each child a copy of photocopiable page 155 to complete.

When the children have finished the photocopiable exercise, ask if they will pretend to be in a story about some gardeners who applied for a job in a palace garden

belonging to a king. Read out the job advert (see above) and ask the children to draw some pictures or plans after discussing some possibilities as a whole class first.

Session Two

Ask the children to pretend that, because of their good ideas, they have all been offered jobs to help make the King's garden of shapes. Ask them to imagine that the hall is the palace garden. Define the areas to be used in the drama and make it clear that the children will need to mime the gardening. Explain that you will pretend to be the head gardener when you put on the jacket.

Now take on the role of the head gardener and welcome the children as new gardeners, but explain that there is a problem. Sit everyone in a circle around the pile of shapes. Explain that the King has gone away to visit his son and will be back tomorrow, but you will be in trouble if the King's new garden of shapes is not ready by the time he returns. Point to the two labels saying 'Cubes and cuboids' and 'Curves'. Explain that the King wants two models in his new garden: one made of cubes and cuboids and one made of shapes with curves. The pieces for the models have been delivered, but they are all mixed up and you don't know which shapes should go in which models.

Invite the children to help you sort out the pile of 3D shapes. Warn them to handle the shapes carefully. Organize

DRAMA

them into pairs and let each pair put one shape next to the correct label while the rest watch. Encourage the class to help each pair decide where their shape should go. Now arrange everyone to sit in front of the pile of cubes and cuboids. Ask the children how these shapes might be arranged to make an interesting model. Choose some children to arrange the shapes accordingly. Repeat this activity with the curved shapes. Thank the children for their help and admire the models.

Move on to suggest that the gardeners now start on the rest of the garden. Explain that the King wants them to plant some red flowers in the shape of a large circle. Ask everyone to stand in a circle to see where they should plant the flowers. Before they set to work, tell the gardeners how impressed you were with the pictures and plans they sent you and ask them to remind you what else they wanted to put in the garden of shapes. Encourage them to keep to the theme of shapes wherever possible.

Now show the children an imaginary shed where the tools and plants are kept and let them carry out the work by miming the jobs. When most appear to have finished, thank the new gardeners for their work and tell them that they will be sent their pay tomorrow, when the King returns. Take off the jacket to come out of role and tell the children that when the King returned, he was so pleased with his garden that he sent the gardeners some extra money. Explain that this is the end of the story.

Look at the models again and talk about how the shapes for these were sorted. Let the children dismantle the models a shape at a time. Take photographs of each of the models before dismantling them.

Suggestion(s) for extension

When dismantling the models, ask confident children to pick out the shapes by name, for example: 'Take out a sphere/cylinder/cube/cuboid' or use other mathematical criteria such as 'Take out a shape that has corners/no corners'. Encourage these children to think of ideas for the garden that are consistent with the shapes theme. Ask groups to role play taking the King on a guided tour of the garden. This can be performed as a spontaneous improvisation in front of the class at the end of the story.

Suggestion(s) for support

Pair up those children who need support with more confident children when sorting the shapes. Work alongside less confident children as the head gardener.

Assessment opportunities

Look for any children who can identify the individual 3D shapes by name and those who can sort them appropriately. Note any children who express imaginative ideas for making a garden with a shape theme and those who mime the gardening with accuracy and integrity.

Opportunities for IT

The children could use an art or drawing package to create their own models from cubes, cuboids and curves. They will need to know

Palace Weekly Newspaper

GARDENERS WANTED

Do you know something about shapes? If you do, we need you to help us in the King's new garden of shapes. The King wants his new garden to be different from other gardens, and wants everything in it to be about shapes. We are looking for gardeners who have good ideas and who know something about shapes. If you are interested in the job, please send us a plan or a picture of your ideas for a garden of shapes as soon as possible.

Send your ideas to: The Head Gardener, Palace Gardens, Royal Square, Shapestown.

how to create the shapes, stretch and shrink them and move them around the screen. They will also need to know how to colour the shapes. Similar activities can be undertaken with framework software such as *My World*, where the children are given a set of shapes to begin with and can arrange them to make other shapes.

Display ideas
Display the original pictures and plans for a shapes garden alongside a copy of the advert. Add the photographs of the models.

Reference to photocopiable sheet
Photocopiable page 155 reinforces the children's knowledge of the mathematical terms which are used in the main activity.

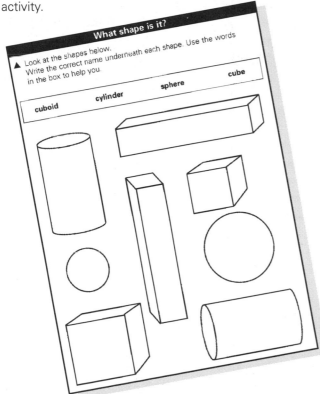

GRAVITY

To use whole-group drama to introduce children to a historical figure.

†† *Whole-class and pairs.*

🕐 *45 minutes.*

Previous skills/knowledge needed
The children should be familiar with the word 'gravity' and have some understanding of the effects of gravity on everyday things.

Key background knowledge
This activity focuses on some basic facts about the life of Isaac Newton and the effects of gravity when travelling in space. It attempts to teach the historical facts about Isaac Newton through using teacher-in-role as a key strategy. The activity requires a large space, but the introduction can take place in the classroom.

Preparation
Make one copy photocopiable page 156 per pair of children. Make a sign saying 'Woolsthorpe Manor Cottage and Farm' and put this on a chair.

Resources needed
Photocopiable page 156, a large space, a sheet of A4 card, a felt-tipped pen, a chair, a scarf or shawl to represent an English farm worker in 1660, a whistle, a book, pencil, sheet of paper and tissue for each pair of children.

What to do
Organize the children into pairs and give each pair a copy of photocopiable page 156 to complete. Use this to remind the children about the effects of gravity on everyday things.

Follow this by asking the children to go back a long way in time to the year 1660, to help gather apples on a farm. Talk about what life would have been like then and stress the absence of modern appliances. Make it clear that they will need to mime picking up the apples. Point to the sign on the chair saying 'Woolsthorpe Manor Cottage and Farm' and ask the children to pretend that this area of the hall is the farm. Explain that they have come to work for a Mrs Newton, who owns the farm with her son Isaac. Tell them that you will pretend to be Mrs Newton or one of Mrs Newton's farm workers when you put on the scarf.

Take on the role of Mrs Newton (or a farm worker) and mime picking up apples from beneath the apple trees, looking very tired and unhappy while you do this. Look over to the children and look pleased to see them. Tell them that you are glad to get some help on the farm because Isaac won't help you. Explain how clever Isaac is and how he has been sent home from University because many people there are ill with a sickness called the Plague. Tell them how he is always dreaming and thinking about things instead of helping on the farm.

Now explain how one day, when Isaac was helping to pick up the apples, he suddenly ran inside and started writing. Say that this was how Isaac discovered gravity, and explain this at a level appropriate to the needs of the class. Talk about how amazed you are that you can't actually see gravity, and yet Isaac has shown you that it is there because the apples always fall down from the tree to the ground. Explain that Isaac is inside the cottage at the moment writing letters to everyone to tell them about gravity, so he will not help you with the apples.

Finish by asking the children if they will help to pick up the apples from beneath the trees and put them in sacks. As the children mime this, keep mentioning how amazed

Suggestion(s) for extension

Ask the more confident children to do some research on the effects of gravity on astronauts in space ships. Encourage them to mime some situations showing how astronauts cope with everyday tasks such as eating food and cleaning their teeth. They can make this amusing by showing what happens when things float away.

Suggestion(s) for support

Prepare less confident children for the drama by giving them plenty of opportunity to carry out simple experiments which demonstrate gravity. Make sure they are familiar with the term 'gravity' and look at pictures of spaceships prior to the drama. Put these children in pairs to complete the movement activity.

you are that gravity has made the apples fall from the tree. After a short while, thank the children for their help and take off the scarf to come out of role.

Next, explain that there was a real person called Isaac Newton who discovered gravity over 400 years ago. Ask the children what they can remember about Isaac Newton. After a few minutes, move on to talk about the absence of gravity in space and how this makes everything float around. Talk about how astronauts need heavy space boots to keep their feet on the ground and discuss how the absence of gravity makes them move slowly.

Now ask the children to find a space and try to walk like an astronaut in heavy boots. Next let them pretend to be an astronaut fixing a computer. Talk about how the tools would float about if they let them go, and ask them to let this happen a few times as they perform the task. Encourage them to move slowly with floating movements. Finish by asking them to mime working in an imaginary space ship, sometimes slowly working on the computers and sometimes fetching tools to fix them. Let the children perform these movements to each other, half the class at a time.

Assessment opportunities

Look for children who are able to recall what they have been told about Isaac Newton in the drama. Note those children who respond appropriately in role and can work alongside others in a whole-group situation. Look for children who can consistently use slow movements, as if they were in space.

Opportunities for IT

The children could use a science or encyclopaedia CD-ROM to research other information about Isaac Newton or gravity. They could combine the information they have found into a fact sheet about Isaac Newton, with each child or group adding one or two different facts about his life and work.

They could also use the word processor to write a poem, perhaps entitled 'Without Gravity'. A simple poem structure could be set up to provide a framework for the writing.

Display ideas

Make some models of space rockets and collect pictures of farm life in the 1600s. Display these items with information about Isaac Newton to stimulate discussion and recall the events in the drama.

Reference to photocopiable sheet

Photocopiable page 156 is used as an introduction to focus and extend the children's thinking about gravity in preparation for the drama.

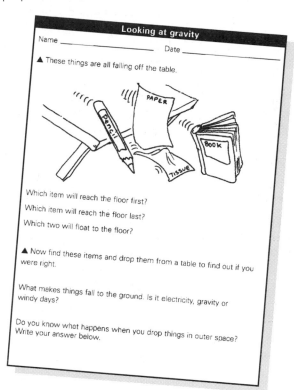

NUMBERS IN ACTION

To use physical theatre to represent numbers and simple sums.

✝✝ *Whole class.*

🕐 *20 to 30 minutes.*

Previous skills/knowledge needed

Children should be able to recognize the numbers 1 to 10 and should be familiar with the plus, minus and equal signs. They should also have some basic movement experience.

Key background knowledge

This activity uses the body to reinforce number recognition and facilitate group work on addition and subtraction. The mathematics can be adapted to suit the needs of the group.

Preparation

Write out the numbers one to ten on separate cards. Write out the plus, minus and equals signs on separate cards in a different colour to that used for the numbers. Make one copy of photocopiable page 157 and glue this to a stiff sheet of A4 card.

Resources needed

Photocopiable page 157, a large space, thirteen A4 sheets of card, glue, felt-tipped pens in two different colours, a tambour.

What to do

Gather the children to sit in front of you. Hold up the number one and ask if someone will show the class how to make this shape with their body. Let one child demonstrate, then move on to the number two. Let individual children demonstrate suggestions on how to represent each number using their body. Use two children to represent the shape for number ten.

Next, move on to making the shapes of the mathematical signs. Show the children the ideas on the photocopiable sheet (stuck onto card) and ask them to demonstrate their own ideas if they are significantly different from those on the sheet. Make it clear that there may be more than one way of making a number or a sign with the body.

Now tell the children to find a space and sit down to face you, making sure they can all see you. Explain that when you hold up a card with a number on, everyone must say the number and then make the shape of that number with their bodies. When you bang the tambour, they must come out of the shape and sit down. Go through the numbers in order and pair children up for the number ten. Pair with a child yourself if there is an

and the children shape their bodies along the lines to make the numbers on the floor. Involve the less able children at a level they can cope with during the sums activities. Ask them to make the simpler numbers when recreating the sums and give them an opportunity to hold up and call out the cards. You can also involve them by inviting them to think of the first number for a new sum that you are making up.

Assessment opportunities
Look for children who are physically confident and those who make imaginative and accurate attempts to represent the numbers and signs. Look for those who respond quickly and accurately to the mathematics involved.

Performance ideas
New sums can be written out on cards and performed to a wider audience for assemblies or for other classes.

Reference to photocopiable sheet
Photocopiable page 157 is intended to help the children visualize how to make the shapes of numbers and mathematical signs using their bodies.

odd number. Then call out a few numbers without showing the cards and tell the children to make the shapes quickly with their bodies each time.

Next, stand with the children in a large semi-circle and ask them to sit down. Use the space in front of the semi-circle for all the following activities. Bring out five cards and let children hold them up at the front to make a simple sum, such as 1 + 2 = 3. Ask five children to enter the space at the front, one at a time, to make the number and sign shapes so that they create the sum with their bodies. Let them chant the sum when it is complete. Repeat the activity with a few more sums, including those involving subtraction. Use pairs to make double numbers. Once the children are confident with this, leave out the answer card and ask them to work this out before someone makes the shape. Finally, let the children make up their own sums for the activity.

Suggestion(s) for extension
For the more confident children, miss out other parts of sums as well as the answers and ask for their suggestions as to the missing part. Include multiplication and division signs to make more complicated sums for the children to act out. Ask pairs to work out a sequence of movements showing different ways of going from one number to the next when performing the numbers one to ten.

Suggestion(s) for support
Encourage less confident children to watch each other to help them decide how to make the number shapes. If necessary, make the number shapes with string or chalk

Photocopiables

The pages in this section can be photocopied for use in the classroom or school which has purchased this book, and do not need to be declared in any return in respect of any photocopying licence.

They comprise a varied selection of both pupil and teacher resources, including pupil worksheets and resource material. All the photocopiable pages are related to individual activities in the book; the name of the activity is indicated at the top of the sheet, together with a page reference indicating where the lesson plan for that activity can be found.

Individual pages are discussed in detail within each lesson plan, accompanied by ideas for adaptation where appropriate – of course, each sheet can be adapted to suit your own needs and those of your class. Sheets can also be coloured, laminated, mounted onto card, enlarged and so on where appropriate.

Pupil worksheets have spaces provided for children's names and for noting the date on which each sheet was used. This means that, if so required, they can be included easily within any pupil assessment portfolio.

Photocopiables

What are they thinking?

Name _____   Date _____

▲Use the speech bubbles to write each character's thoughts.

Humpty Dumpty

Baby Bear

Little Miss Muffett

The third Little Pig

DRAMA

Sound shapes, see page 15

Find the initials

Name _____ Date _____

These children don't know their initials. Can you help them?
▲ Write their initials beneath their names.

David Harrison

Joanne Rutledge

Martin Shaw

Sabina Patel

Gareth Ben Davies

Vincent Young

Patrick Ian Wood

Elaine Leung

Write your own initials.

DRAMA

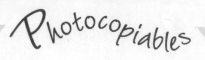

Who's my character?

Name _____   Date _____

▲ Write the name of your character here. _____

▲ Draw a picture of your character in the box.

▲ Write three things you know about your character.

1. _____

2. _____

3. _____

▲ What is your character like? Circle the words that describe your character.

kind	unkind	funny	silly	friendly	naughty
shy	clever	bad	greedy	good	sad

▲ Draw a picture of something that happened to your character in the story.

▲ Talk to your partner about what happened to your character in the story.

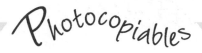

Sequencing a story, see page 21

Little Red Riding Hood

Section 1: The children play the part of Little Red Riding Hood.

▲ Little Red Riding Hood waved goodbye to her mother and set off on the path through the forest to take a basket of food to her sick grandma. On the way, she left the path to pick some flowers for her grandma.
Opportunities for mime: *waving goodbye, walking, picking flowers.*

Section 2: The children play the part of Little Red Riding Hood.

▲ Little Red Riding Hood met a wolf who asked her where she was going. She told the wolf the way to her grandma's house and carried on picking flowers.
Opportunities for mime: *pointing the way to Grandma's house, picking flowers.*

Section 3: The children play the part of the wolf.

▲ The wolf ran to Grandma's house and knocked on the door. Grandma thought it was Little Red Riding Hood and told him to lift the latch and come inside. The wolf went into Grandma's house and Grandma, realizing her mistake, hid in a cupboard feeling very frightened. The wolf dressed up in some of Grandma's clothes and sat in her bed. He pulled the bed covers over his face.
Opportunities for mime: *running to the house, knocking on the door, entering the house, dressing up in Grandma's clothes, getting into bed, pulling up the bed covers.*

Section 4: The children play the part of the wolf.

▲ When Little Red Riding Hood came in, she thought the wolf was her grandma. The wolf sprang out of bed and chased Little Red Riding Hood round the house and out into the forest.
Opportunities for mime: *jumping out of bed, chasing round furniture, chasing outside among the trees.*

Section 5: The children play the part of the woodcutter.

▲ A woodcutter heard Little Red Riding Hood shouting for help. He chased the wolf and caught it in a big sack. He tied the sack with some rope and took the wolf to the zoo.
Opportunities for mime: *chasing the wolf, putting the wolf in the sack, tying the sack, carrying the wolf to the zoo.*

Section 6: The children play the part of Little Red Riding Hood.

▲ Little Red Riding Hood said thank you to the woodcutter and waved goodbye to him as he went off to the zoo. She went into the house and let Grandma out of the cupboard. She helped Grandma back into bed and gave her the food she had brought in her basket. She also gave her the flowers she had picked. 'I'm feeling much better now,' said Grandma, and Little Red Riding Hood smiled a great big smile.
Opportunities for mime: *waving to the woodcutter, opening the cupboard, helping Grandma into bed, giving Grandma some food, giving Grandma the flowers, smiling.*

Journey to storyland, see page 23

The house of bricks

DRAMA

Journey to storyland, see page 23

Clothes for storyland (1)

Clothes for storyland (1)

DRAMA

Clothes for storyland (2)

DRAMA

Journey to storyland, see page 23

On the way to storyland

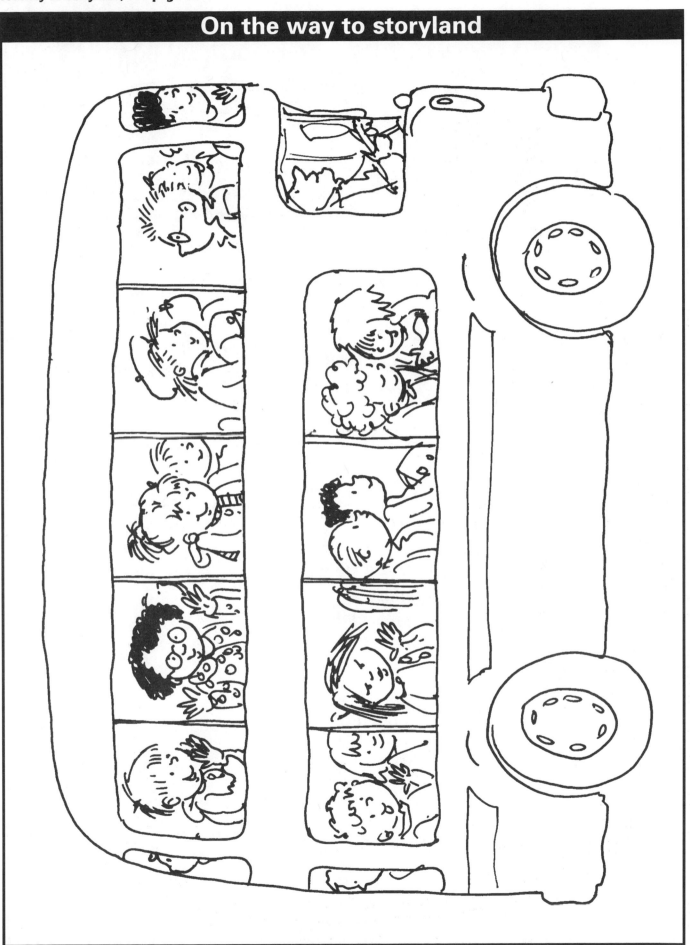

DRAMA

Journey to storyland, see page 23

A letter from storyland

The Brick House,
3 Green Lane,
Storyland

Dear children,
I am sorry I am not at home, but I have gone to tell Mummy Pig what happened when the wolf tried to blow my house down.

She has been very worried about me since she heard that there was a wolf near Green Lane. There are no more wolves now and so you will all be safe.

I would like to ask for your help. My new house of bricks needs decorating. I am not very good at decorating and I was wondering if you could do some of it for me while I am at my mother's house. Everything you need is in the garden shed. Thank you so much.

Love from the third Little Pig

DRAMA

A garden for Snow White, see page 28

Radio Palace: listeners' letters

Dear Radio Palace,

I would like to ask the planners what flowers they have put in Snow White's garden.

From Robert Green

- -

Dear Radio Palace,

I would like to know if there is anywhere in the garden for Snow White to find shade from the sun on a hot day. Thank you.

From Kerry Harris

- -

Dear Radio Palace,

Please could your special guests tell me where Snow White will be able to sit in the garden and if there is anywhere she could have a picnic. Thank you.

From Mr Charles Jackman

- -

Dear Radio Palace,

Please would you ask the planners if they have put any buildings in Snow White's garden and if so, what are they for.

From Mrs Doris Shaw

- -

Dear Radio Palace,

I have seen the gardeners working in the garden and they say it's the best garden they have ever made. Please would you ask the planners what are their favourite parts of the garden and why? Thank you.

From Aqueel Hassani

- -

Dear Radio Palace,

If Snow White has any children to stay in her palace, will there be anywhere for them to play in the garden? Please will you ask the planners. Thank you.

From Benjamin Wood

- -

Dear Radio Palace,

If Snow White and the Prince are in the garden and it starts to rain, will there be anywhere for them to shelter? Please will you ask your special guests. Thank you.

From Mrs White

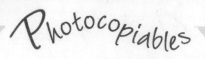

I don't know how to, see page 31

How is it done?

Name _____ Date _____

Work on your own or with a partner.

▲ List 3 things you need to do to paint a picture.
Use these words to help you.

mix paint water paintpot paintbrush paper easel dry

1. _____
2. _____
3. _____

△ Use your list to help you mime painting a picture.

△ List 4 things you do when you shop at the supermarket. Use these
words to help you.

trolley packet box carton bottle wait checkout pay money car

1. _____
2. _____
3. _____
4. _____

△ Use your list to help you mime shopping at the supermarket.

△ List 4 things you might do when you buy some new shoes. Use
these words to help you.

measure size try on walk pay carry box bag

1. _____
2. _____
3. _____
4. _____

▲ Use your list to help you mime buying some new shoes.

DRAMA

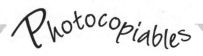

The lost dog, see page 33

All about my dog

Name _____   Date _____

▲ Draw a picture of your lost dog in the space below.

▲ Now answer these questions about your lost dog.
Think about your answers and write some of them down if you wish.

What is your dog's name?

Was your dog wearing a collar with a name tag?

What colour is your dog?

How big is your dog?

Does your dog have long hair or short hair?

Does your dog have long legs or short legs?

How did you lose your dog?

How long has your dog been missing?

Sort out the sequence

Name _____ Date _____

These pictures are in the wrong order and one is missing.
▲ Draw a line from the sentence to the correct picture.
   Then draw in the missing picture.

Hamelin was full of rats.

The Mayor offered a reward.

The Pied Piper led the rats to the river.

The Mayor would not give the
Pied Piper his money.

The Pied Piper led the children away.

Let's mime it!, see page 44

The garden

Once upon a time there was a woman who had a garden. There was no fence round her garden. All the rubbish blew in and made the garden look untidy. The woman was sad because she had no fence.

One day, her friends arrived with hammers and nails and pieces of wood. They built a lovely fence round her garden.
Children mime building the fence.

The woman liked her fence, but she was still sad. The next day, the wind blew through the garden, but the fence was strong and did not blow down.
Children move to represent the wind (for example, wavy arm movements).

Then the rain fell on the garden.
Children move to represent the rain falling (for example, wriggling fingers from high to low like raindrops falling).

Then the sun shone on the garden.
Children move to represent sun shining (for example, spreading arms wide).

But still the woman was sad. She was sad because she had no flowers in her garden. One day, her friends came with garden tools and flowers and planted them round the edge of the woman's fence.
Children mime planting flowers round the fence.

When the woman saw the beautiful flowers in her garden, she was very happy. She invited her friends to walk round her garden and look at the flowers.
Children stand up and walk round the garden to look at the imaginary flowers.

...and everyone was happy.
Children sit down.

A day at the park

▲ Use these pictures to help you make up a play about a day at the park.

1. Playing ball on the grass.

2. Feeding the ducks.

3. Rowing a boat.

4. Playing on the swings.

5. Buying and eating an ice cream.

6. Looking at the flowers.

Shopping centre, see page 49

Which shop?

Name _____ Date _____

Part A
Where would you buy each of the items below?
▲ Join up the words to the correct shop. An example has been done for you.

teddy
sandals
wellington boots
toy car
ball
trainers
boxed game
doll
slippers
football boots

Toy Shop

Shoe Shop

▲ Write three things you will ask for when you pretend to visit the toy shop.

1.

2.

3.

Part B
▲ What size shoes will you ask for when you pretend to visit the shoe shop?

▲ What kind of shoes will you ask for?

▲ Will you ask for shoes with laces, buckles or velcro?

DRAMA

Moving pictures, see page 52

In the playground

▲ Make a freeze-frame of all or part of this picture and bring it to life for a short time. Finish with another freeze-frame.

DRAMA

Moving pictures, see page 52

Birthday party

▲ Make a freeze-frame of all or part of this picture and bring it to life for a short time. Finish with another freeze-frame.

DRAMA

Rehearsing the school play, see page 55

Rehearsal grid

Date and time	Place	Rehearsal unit number and brief description	Names of characters or groups of characters

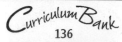

Puppets on the move, see page 58

Puppet play: Sun, rain and wind

One sunny day *(name the puppets)* decided to go for a walk. It was very hot and so they walked very slowly.

(Pause until the first puppet reaches the end of the sheet.)

Suddenly, it started to rain, so they ran back home as quickly as they could.

(Let all the puppets go off the stage.)

The next day, it was cold and windy, but *(name the puppets)* decided to go for a walk anyway. Then it started to rain. They were feeling very sad without the sun. Suddenly, a strange thing happened. The wind died down, the rain stopped and the sun came out.

(Name the puppets) were feeling very happy as they walked back home in the sunshine. As they looked up at the sky, they saw a lovely rainbow. But they were not looking where they were going and suddenly, they all fell over and started to cry. They decided to sing a little song to cheer themselves up.

(Choose a song about the weather such as 'I Hear Thunder' by Max De Bóo, Scholastic.)

Soon they felt a lot better and set off home feeling happy again. In fact they were so happy that every now and again, they gave a little jump to show just how good they felt about seeing the sun again. And that is the end of the story.

(Let all puppets go off stage and then reappear to take a bow as the class applaud them.)

Watching theatre, see page 60

Costumes

Name _____ Date _____

▲ Draw and colour a costume for each of these actors and actresses.

I am going to be a queen.

I am going to be a teacher.

I am going to be Red Riding Hood.

I am going to be a fireman.

Puppets with problems, see page 64

How do they feel? (1)

HAPPINESS

SADNESS

DRAMA

Puppets with problems, see page 64

How do they feel? (2)

ANGER

FEAR

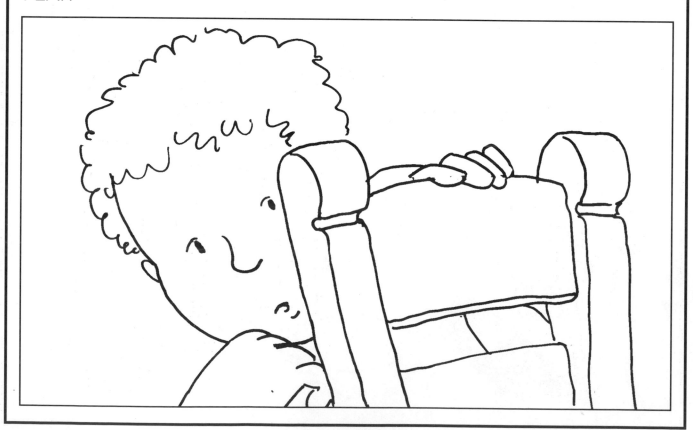

Bullies in focus, see page 66

What's happening? (1)

DRAMA

Bullies in focus, see page 66

What's happening? (2)

DRAMA

Grandad's garden, see page 74

The story of Grandad's garden

Gemma's grandad was feeling very sad.

(Grandad puts on the scarf and sits in his chair looking sad.)

His new bungalow had no garden. There was a small patch of bare earth in front of his window, but that was all. One day, Gemma brought some seeds and some gardening tools to Grandad's bungalow.

(Gemma puts on her coat and mimes carrying the tools to the centre of the circle.)

She went to the small patch of earth outside Grandad's window and planted the seeds.

(Gemma mimes planting the seeds and then returns to circle. The child chosen as the seed moves to where Gemma has been planting and curls up tightly.)

As the days passed, the rain fell on the bare earth outside Grandad's window.

(Gemma and Grandad play tambourines as the class make rain movements.)

The sun shone on the bare earth outside Grandad's window.

(Children make sun movements, reaching over towards the seed. Gemma and Grandad play the tambourines.)

One day, one of the seeds began to grow *(child who is the seed starts to move upwards)*. As the days passed, it grew bigger.

(Let two children extend the plant by joining themselves to the child's arms. They should do this by gently making contact with part of the child's arm using their fingers.)

And it grew bigger.

(Repeat this phrase pointing to various children each time, as a signal that they must join on to an extended arm to make the plant spread outwards. Ask them to join on arms at both ends of the plant, so that it grows in both directions. They should make the plant grow in a curve rather than in a line.)

The plant was so big that it covered the bare earth outside Grandad's window. Then insects flew among the leaves of the plant. *(Insects fly around.)* Then birds flew around the plant *(birds fly around)*, and after that, some cats came to lie in the shade of the plant *(cats creep under the leaves)*. When Grandad looked out of his window he was really pleased. He went to his cupboard, took out a small watering can and filled it with water from the tap.

(Grandad looks pleased and steps into the edge of the circle to mime the actions.)

He took the watering can to the piece of earth outside his window and watered the plant. *(Grandad walks around the plant to water it.)*

When Gemma came back to visit, Grandad smiled a great big smile, and so did Gemma.

(Gemma arrives and they both smile.)

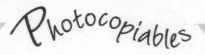
Jobs on the farm

Name _____   Date _____

Here are some farm jobs:

collecting eggs	loading hay	milking cows	shearing sheep
feeding animals	fixing tractors	cleaning out the animals	dipping sheep
ploughing fields	mending fences		hoeing vegetables

▲ Pretend that you work on a small farm. What job do you do ?

▲ Draw a picture of what you do on the farm.

▲ Now write about your job here. Fill in the gaps below.

I work on a small farm. My job is to _____

This is how I do my job:

First I _____

Next I _____

Then I _____

The lonely prince, see page 80

Preparing for the prince's party

Name _____ Date _____

Here is a list of things the servants need for the prince's party.

Food

large cakes	rolls
small cakes	pies
sandwiches	flans
fruit and jelly	pop
biscuits	orange squash
crisps	
food on sticks	
pasties	

Equipment

plates	chairs
dishes	tablecloths
cups	cocktail sticks
drinking glasses	candles
straws	balloons
spoons	decorations
cake	scissors
knives	sticky tape
tables	ladder

▲ Now choose three jobs that you will do in the kitchen and write them here.

1. _____

2. _____

3. _____

Describe how you will do these jobs. Write in the boxes below, using the words to help you.

make bake mix cut put stick blow wash clean whisk stir open find lay set

Job 1

Job 2

Job 3

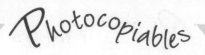

Friendship

Name _____ Date _____

Which of these children are Sam's friends?

▲ Read these sentences and tick in the boxes next to the names of the children who are his friends.

Dean shares his sweets with Sam on the way home from school.	**Dean**	☐
Mary laughs when Sam gets things wrong.	**Mary**	☐
Shamina helps Sam with his work.	**Shamina**	☐
Ben pushes in front of Sam when they line up at school.	**Ben**	☐
Joanne teases Sam because he wears glasses.	**Joanne**	☐
Kate asks Sam to play with her when he is on his own.	**Kate**	☐
Tom stays with Sam when he is feeling sad.	**Tom**	☐
Richard always listens to what Sam has to say.	**Richard**	☐
Lucy won't let Sam sit next to her at school.	**Lucy**	☐

▲ Write three things that good friends do for each other.

1. _____

2. _____

3. _____

Santa's helpers, see page 84

Finish the toys

Name _____ Date _____

▲ These toys are not finished. Draw a line to join up the right parts to the toys.

bike

rocking horse

teddy

slide

car

doll

▲ Which toys are wrapped in these Christmas parcels? Draw a line from the picture to the right parcel.

Letters from Santa

Santa's toy shop

Dear children,
Please will you help me. I have almost finished making the toys to take to children on Christmas Eve, but last night I caught a bad cold and I have had to go to bed. My helpers have all got colds too, and there is no one to finish the toys. If the toys are not finished soon, children will have no presents on Christmas day. I have sent you the key to my shop. All the tools you will need are in the shop. I have also sent you a sleigh to take you to my shop. All you need to do to get to my shop is to sit on the sleigh and sing 'Jingle Bells'. It will also bring you safely back again when you have finished the toys. Please help me.

Love from Santa

✄ -- Cut
here

Santa's toy shop

Dear children,
Thank you very much for finishing the toys in my toy shop and wrapping the small presents. That will save me time on Christmas Eve. I am feeling much better now and I am back in the toy shop, loading the toys onto my sleigh. Rudolph says hello to you all. I think you must be some of the kindest children I know. Thank you for making me so happy. Have a happy Christmas.

Love from Santa

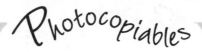
Kites and washing, see page 94

A windy day

Name _____ Date _____

▲ Fill in the spaces to tell the story about what happened on the windy day.

1. We went out to fly our kites on a cold, _____(windy, rainy, snowy, sunny) day.

2. We packed our kites into our_____(bags, pockets).

3. The wind made us walk _____(quickly, slowly).

4. We found a _____ (bus, flower, tree) that had been blown down by the wind.

5. We flew our_____ (kites, planes) in the wind.

6. We sang a song about the_____(sun, snow, wind).

7. Some washing had blown into the _____(pond, bushes, house).

8. We found the washing and put it in a _____ (box, shed, greenhouse).

9. The wind had blown down a _____(house, fence, wall).

10. We mended the fence using hammers and _____(pins, bricks, nails).

▲ Draw a picture of the washing you found in the bushes.

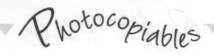

Jean's war, see page 97

Life in wartime

Name _____   Date _____

▲ Look carefully at the toys below.
Put a tick next to the toys that children played with in the war.

| skipping-rope | walkman | marbles | computer | ball | rollerblades |

▲ Now fill in the spaces in Jean's school book.

My name is Jean and I am _____ years old.

My dad is away from home. He has gone to _____ .

My mum works in a nursery. She looks after _____ .

I like to play games with my younger brothers and sisters.

The games I like to play are _____ .

We go down an air raid shelter to keep us safe from the _____ .

When we are down the shelter we feel very _____ .

I sing to my brothers and sisters to cheer them up. One nursery rhyme

I like to sing is called _____ .

DRAMA

Jean's war, see page 97

Leaving home

Name _____ Date _____

▲ What did you pack in your bag to remind you of home?

_____

_____

▲ How did you feel when you packed your bag?

_____

_____

▲ Below are some evacuee children on a train during the war. Fill in the thought bubbles to show what they are thinking.

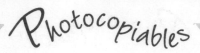

Shepherds, angels, and a star, see page 102

What are they thinking?

Name _____ Date _____

▲ Look at the pictures below. What are the people thinking?

▲ Use the thought bubbles to write in your ideas.

All about my creature

Name _____ Date _____

▲ Write the name of your chosen creature, and then fill in the rest of the information sheet.

Wildlife Park information sheet for a _____

▲ What kind of creature is it (for example, animal, bird, insect, reptile)?

What does it eat?

Which creatures are its enemies?

Which country does it come from?

How dangerous is it?

Is it scared of people?

How do the park workers look after it?

▲ Draw a picture here to show what the creature looks like.

Healthy living, see page 108

Which foods are healthy?

Name _____ Date _____

▲ Which child is eating a healthy lunch today?
Is it Kate, Mark or Kieran?

Which of these foods belong on the supermarket's healthy food shelf?

▲ Draw a line to join up the healthy foods to the shelves.

Fruit

Chocolate

Crisps

Vegetables

Ice cream

Bread

Biscuits

Cakes

Healthy food shelves

▲ Now act out shopping for healthy food with your partner, and eating some of the food at home.

The garden of shapes, see page 111

What shape is it?

▲ Look at the shapes below.
Write the correct name underneath each shape. Use the words in the box to help you.

cuboid	cylinder	sphere	cube

DRAMA

Gravity, see page 113

Looking at gravity

Name _____   Date _____

▲ These things are all falling off the table.

Which item will reach the floor first?

Which item will reach the floor last?

Which two will float to the floor?

▲ Now find these items and drop them from a table to find out if you were right.

What makes things fall to the ground. Is it electricity, gravity or windy days?

Do you know what happens when you drop things in outer space? Write your answer below.

Numbers in action, see page 115

Number shapes

 **1**

 **2**

 **3**

 **4**

 **5**

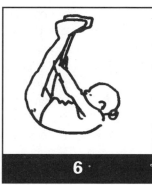 **6**

 **7**

 **8**

 **9**

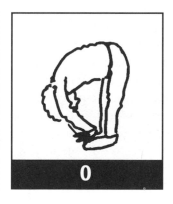 **0**

 **+**

 **−**

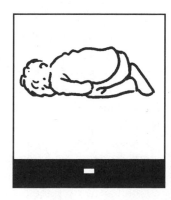 **=**

DRAMA

INFORMATION TECHNOLOGY WITHIN DRAMA

Main IT Focus

The information technology activities outlined in this book can be used to develop and assess children's IT capability as outlined in the National Curriculum. The main emphasis for the development of IT capability within these activities is on communicating information mainly through the combination of text and pictures. This section deals with some of these issues in more detail.

Word processing

Many of the writing activities and extension ideas in this book can be used to develop children's IT capability through the use of a word processor. Of course, not every child has to undertake every suggested writing task using the computer. The teacher could organize children to do different writing tasks over a term or longer, some using more conventional written methods and others using the computer. This would also provide an opportunity for teachers to provide activities at different levels of IT capability and to discuss with different children the relative merits of the use of IT for different purposes.

Throughout Key Stage 1 children should develop their confidence and competence to use word processing or simple desktop publishing packages. Many word processors now have basic desktop publishing features and it may be possible to use a single piece of software for most writing tasks. An important difference between the two types of software is the way in which text is placed on the page. In a desk top publishing package text is generally placed inside a frame which can be moved around the page and altered in size and shape with the text automatically fitting to the new shape. This provides a flexible way for children to organize text and pictures on a page and to experiment with different types of page design. By the end of this Key Stage the children should be able to:

▲ know the layout of the keyboard and use their thumbs to press the space bar

▲ make capital letters and characters found above the number keys by using the shift key

▲ use the delete key to erase words and letters and join lines together

▲ use the cursor/arrow keys or mouse to position the cursor at the desired position

▲ use more than a single finger/hand when typing, particularly as they become more proficient and know where letters and numbers are located

▲ know the word processor will 'wrap' the text around the end of the line without them using the return key

▲ force a new line by using the return key

▲ select an appropriate font from a menu and alter the size and/or colour of single letters, words or lines

▲ centre text using the centre command

▲ add a picture to their work and position and resize it

▲ move the cursor to a mistake and correct it, rather than deleting all the text back to the mistake

▲ print out their completed work, initially with support from the teacher, but eventually on their own.

Children will also need to save their work if they are unable to finish it in one session. They should be taught how to do this onto the hard or floppy disc or network so that eventually they can do it without teacher assistance. They will then need to be shown how to locate and retrieve their work at a later date.

Young children will take a long time to enter text at the keyboard so it is important to ensure that the writing tasks are kept short and that where possible there is additional support available to assist the child's development. It is also useful to have parents or other adults assisting children in editing and re-drafting their work.

Most word processors now have the ability to deal with pictures. These are usually 'imported' or inserted into the children's writing. The children should be taught how to move the pictures around the screen and resize them to fit. Word processors deal with text and pictures in different ways. Some will automatically 'flow' the text around pictures, with others you can decide how this happens and with the simpler word processors it often has to be done a line at a time. In such cases children will need to know how to use the tab key to move text across the picture or change the margin settings. Where desktop publishing type packages are used the pictures will fit into one frame and the text into another. The frames can be re-sized to fill the spaces or the amount of text available.

Using pictures from other sources

Pictures are used in many of the activities to record freeze-frames. Although these are representative of the children's work they could be recorded and used in other IT based activities such as word processing, graphics, posters and multimedia presentations.

Many schools regularly use a traditional camera to take photographs or activities in school. With the advent of cheap, flat-bed scanners schools are able to turn these conventional photographs into digital images which can be used in a range of different applications. Modern scanners produce high quality results at the best resolutions, but the files created can be very large. Schools need to experiment to find a resolution which creates good, useable images at the lowest memory requirement. Around 200 dpi is a good starting point. Scanners can also be used to create digital pictures of children's own line drawings so that work created away from the computer can be incorporated into computer applications. Other photographs, drawings or pictures can be digitized in the same way.

DRAMA

The grids on this page relate the activities in this book to specific areas of IT and to relevant software resources. Types of software rather than names of specific programs have been listed to enable teachers to use the ideas regardless of the computers to which they have access. The software featured should be available from most good educational software retailers. Teachers may still want to include specific software which addresses the content and understanding of the topics being taught. Activities are referenced by page number rather than by name (bold page numbers indicate activities which have expanded IT content).

AREA OF IT	SOFTWARE	ACTIVITIES (PAGE NOS.)			
		CHAPTER 1	**CHAPTER 2**	**CHAPTER 3**	**CHAPTER 4**
Communicating Info	Word processor	**28**, 31, 33, 37	**55**	67, **80**, 84	**90**,97,102,105,113
Communicating Info	Desktop publishing			**67**, **80**	**108**
Communicating Info	Art/Drawing package	**28**, 33	42, 60	**64**, 84	94, 97, 111, 113
Communicating Info	Authoring software		45		**90**
Information handling	CD-ROMs				**97**, 113
Information handling	Graphing software		71		
Control	Tape recorder		**45**		92
Control	Digital camera		42, **55**	**64**	
Modelling	Framework software	31	42		111, 113
Control	LOGO			**87**	

SOFTWARE TYPE	BBC/MASTER	RISCOS	NIMBUS/186	WINDOWS	MACINTOSH
Word processor	*Folio*	*Pendown* *Desk Top Folio* *Textease*	*All Write* *Write On*	*Word* *Write Away* *Textease* *ClarisWorks*	*Word* *EasyWorks* *ClarisWorks* *Creative Writer*
Desktop publishing		*Pendown DTP* *Ovation* *Textease*		*PagePlus* *Publisher* *Textease*	
Art package	*Picture Builder*	*1st Paint* *Kid Pix* *Dazzle*	*Picture Builder*	*Colour Magic* *Kid Pix 2* *Microsoft Paint*	*Kid Pix 2* *Microsoft Paint* *ClarisWorks*
Drawing software		*Draw* *Vector* *Art Works*	*Picture Builder*	*Dazzle* *ClarisWorks* *Oak Draw* *Genesis*	
Multimedia authoring		*Magpie* *Hyperstudio* *Genesis* *Textease*		*Hyperstudio* *Illuminatus* *Textease*	*Hyperstudio*
Drawing package	*Picture Builder* *Grass*	*Draw* *Picture IT* *Art Works*		*ClarisWorks* *Microsoft Draw* *Sparks*	*ClarisWorks* *Microsoft Draw*
Database		*Junior Pinpoint* *Junior Find IT* *Key Note*	*Grass*	*Junior Find IT* *Information* *Workshop*	*ClarisWorks* *EasyWorks*

DRAMA

	MATHS	SCIENCE	HISTORY	GEOGRAPHY	D&T	IT	ART	MUSIC	RE	PE
LANGUAGE AND LITERACY	Talking about how different types of clocks are used to tell the time.		Thinking about village life in medieval times in Hamelin.	Describing a journey and making a plan of a garden.		Taking photographs. Recording onto an audio cassette.	Painting pictures of clocks. Making a frieze and a model of a garden. Drawing special moments and making letter shapes in sand and dough.	Singing and using percussion in stories and movement.	Acting out part of the story of Rama and Sita.	Making shapes with the body. Walking and moving in imaginary situations.
ACTING FOR AN AUDIENCE				Miming activities at the beach and the park. Talking about shopping centres and farms.	Designing and making a simple glove puppet. Making models of a stage. Designing costumes for actors.	Recording rhymes onto an audio cassette	Drawing pictures of activities on the beach and at the park. Looking closely at pictures to act out moments from them.	Using percussion for sound effects.	Acting out moral dilemmas based on given moments.	Moving in different ways. Miming actions.
PERSONAL AND SOCIAL DEVELOPMENT	Being aware of space and distance in directing robots around obstacles.	Talking, drawing and writing about planting and growing seeds. Talking about different kinds of toys and their parts.				Using remote controlled toys.	Making model robots. Drawing scenes depicting significant moments of emotion and solutions to problems. Drawing imaginary islands.	Singing and using percussion to accompany stories.	Talking about Christmas traditions and helping Santa.	Taking part in a variety of movement activities.
CROSS-CURRICULAR THEMES	Representing numbers. Working out and making up sums. Using and naming 3D shapes.	Talking about how to fly a kite. Learning about gravity and its effect on space travellers. Talking about healthy food and exercise.	Learning about Isaac Newton. Comparing domestic tasks with how they were carried out in the past.	Learning about the effects of windy weather on people and the environment. Drawing maps and thinking about the problems of litter in parks.	Making plans for a garden of shapes.	Using a computer to search for information on past and present. Designing and printing posters.	Making models of space rockets. Drawing figures for the Christmas story. Making a model of a wildlife park.	Using percussion for story and dance/drama.	Acting out parts of the Christmas story in a dance/drama.	Taking part in dance/drama. Using physical theatre. Walking as if in a strong wind.

DRAMA